INTRODUCTION TO
MARKETING

Marketing 101
Cases & Readings

TENTH EDITION

Materials coordinated by

Keith Niedermeier

The Wharton School of the University of Pennsylvania

 **Learning Solutions**

Boston   Burr Ridge, IL   Dubuque, IA   New York   San Francisco
St. Louis   Bangkok   Bogotá   Caracas   Lisbon   London   Madrid   Mexico City   Milan
New Delhi   Paris   Seoul   Singapore   Sydney   Taipei   Toronto

The McGraw-Hill Companies

INTRODUCTION TO MARKETING
Marketing 101
Cases and Readings

1 2 3 4 5 6 7 8 9 0   QSR   QSR   0 9 8

ISBN-13: 978-0-07-729872-2
MHID: 0-07-729872-1

Learning Solutions Specialist: Jill Hogstrom
Production Editor: Lynn Nagel
Cover Photos: Macau-Coke Sign by Keith Niedermeier; Flag by Royalty-Free/CORBIS
Cover Design: Maggie Lytle
Printer/Binder: Quebecor World

Table of Contents

HARVARD │ BUSINESS │ SCHOOL

9-504-016

REV: JULY 10, 2006

YOUNGME MOON

JOHN QUELCH

Starbucks: Delivering Customer Service

In late 2002, Christine Day, Starbucks' senior vice president of administration in North America, sat in the seventh-floor conference room of Starbucks' Seattle headquarters and reached for her second cup of toffee-nut latte. The handcrafted beverage—a buttery, toffee-nut flavored espresso concoction topped with whipped cream and toffee sprinkles—had become a regular afternoon indulgence for Day ever since its introduction earlier that year.

As she waited for her colleagues to join her, Day reflected on the company's recent performance. While other retailers were still reeling from the post-9/11 recession, Starbucks was enjoying its 11th consecutive year of 5% or higher comparable store sales growth, prompting its founder and chairman, Howard Schultz, to declare: "I think we've demonstrated that we are close to a recession-proof product."[1]

Day, however, was not feeling nearly as sanguine, in part because Starbucks' most recent market research had revealed some unexpected findings. "We've always taken great pride in our retail service," said Day, "but according to the data, we're not always meeting our customers' expectations in the area of customer satisfaction."

As a result of these concerns, Day and her associates had come up with a plan to invest an additional $40 million annually in the company's 4,500 stores, which would allow each store to add the equivalent of 20 hours of labor a week. "The idea is to improve speed-of-service and thereby increase customer satisfaction," said Day.

In two days, Day was due to make a final recommendation to both Schultz and Orin Smith, Starbucks' CEO, about whether the company should move forward with the plan. "The investment is the EPS [earnings per share] equivalent of almost seven cents a share," said Day. In preparation for her meeting with Schultz and Smith, Day had asked one of her associates to help her think through the implications of the plan. Day noted, "The real question is, do we believe what our customers are telling us about what constitutes 'excellent' customer service? And if we deliver it, what will the impact be on our sales and profitability?"

---

[1] Jake Batsell, "A Grande Decade for Starbucks," *The Seattle Times*, June 26, 2002.

Company Background

The story of how Howard Schultz managed to transform a commodity into an upscale cultural phenomenon has become the stuff of legends. In 1971, three coffee fanatics—Gerald Baldwin, Gordon Bowker, and Ziev Siegl—opened a small coffee shop in Seattle's Pike Place Market. The shop specialized in selling whole arabica beans to a niche market of coffee purists.

In 1982, Schultz joined the Starbucks marketing team; shortly thereafter, he traveled to Italy, where he became fascinated with Milan's coffee culture, in particular, the role the neighborhood espresso bars played in Italians' everyday social lives. Upon his return, the inspired Schultz convinced the company to set up an espresso bar in the corner of its only downtown Seattle shop. As Schultz explained, the bar became the prototype for his long-term vision:

> The idea was to create a chain of coffeehouses that would become America's "third place."
> At the time, most Americans had two places in their lives—home and work. But I believed
> that people needed another place, a place where they could go to relax and enjoy others, or just
> be by themselves. I envisioned a place that would be separate from home or work, a place that
> would mean different things to different people.

A few years later, Schultz got his chance when Starbucks' founders agreed to sell him the company. As soon as Schultz took over, he immediately began opening new stores. The stores sold whole beans and premium-priced coffee beverages by the cup and catered primarily to affluent, well-educated, white-collar patrons (skewed female) between the ages of 25 and 44. By 1992, the company had 140 such stores in the Northwest and Chicago and was successfully competing against other small-scale coffee chains such as Gloria Jean's Coffee Bean and Barnie's Coffee & Tea.

That same year, Schultz decided to take the company public. As he recalled, many Wall Street types were dubious about the idea: "They'd say, 'You mean, you're going to sell coffee for a dollar in a paper cup, with Italian names that no one in America can say? At a time in America when no one's drinking coffee? And I can get coffee at the local coffee shop or doughnut shop for 50 cents? Are you kidding me?'"[2]

Ignoring the skeptics, Schultz forged ahead with the public offering, raising $25 million in the process. The proceeds allowed Starbucks to open more stores across the nation.

By 2002, Schultz had unequivocally established Starbucks as the dominant specialty-coffee brand in North America. Sales had climbed at a compound annual growth rate (CAGR) of 40% since the company had gone public, and net earnings had risen at a CAGR of 50%. The company was now serving 20 million unique customers in well over 5,000 stores around the globe and was opening on average three new stores a day. (See **Exhibits 1–3** for company financials and store growth over time.)

What made Starbucks' success even more impressive was that the company had spent almost nothing on advertising to achieve it. North American marketing primarily consisted of point-of-sale materials and local-store marketing and was far less than the industry average. (Most fast-food chains had marketing budgets in the 3%–6% range.)

For his part, Schultz remained as chairman and chief global strategist in control of the company, handing over day-to-day operations in 2002 to CEO Orin Smith, a Harvard MBA (1967) who had joined the company in 1990.

---

[2] Batsell.

The Starbucks Value Proposition

Starbucks' brand strategy was best captured by its "live coffee" mantra, a phrase that reflected the importance the company attached to keeping the national coffee culture alive. From a retail perspective, this meant creating an "experience" around the consumption of coffee, an experience that people could weave into the fabric of their everyday lives.

There were three components to this experiential branding strategy. The first component was the coffee itself. Starbucks prided itself on offering what it believed to be the highest-quality coffee in the world, sourced from the Africa, Central and South America, and Asia-Pacific regions. To enforce its exacting coffee standards, Starbucks controlled as much of the supply chain as possible—it worked directly with growers in various countries of origin to purchase green coffee beans, it oversaw the custom-roasting process for the company's various blends and single-origin coffees, and it controlled distribution to retail stores around the world.

The second brand component was service, or what the company sometimes referred to as "customer intimacy." "Our goal is to create an uplifting experience every time you walk through our door," explained Jim Alling, Starbucks' senior vice president of North American retail. "Our most loyal customers visit us as often as 18 times a month, so it could be something as simple as recognizing you and knowing your drink or customizing your drink just the way you like it."

The third brand component was atmosphere. "People come for the coffee," explained Day, "but the ambience is what makes them want to stay." For that reason, most Starbucks had seating areas to encourage lounging and layouts that were designed to provide an upscale yet inviting environment for those who wanted to linger. "What we have built has universal appeal," remarked Schultz. "It's based on the human spirit, it's based on a sense of community, the need for people to come together."[3]

Channels of Distribution

Almost all of Starbucks' locations in North America were company-operated stores located in high-traffic, high-visibility settings such as retail centers, office buildings, and university campuses.[4] In addition to selling whole-bean coffees, these stores sold rich-brewed coffees, Italian-style espresso drinks, cold-blended beverages, and premium teas. Product mixes tended to vary depending on a store's size and location, but most stores offered a variety of pastries, sodas, and juices, along with coffee-related accessories and equipment, music CDs, games, and seasonal novelty items. (About 500 stores even carried a selection of sandwiches and salads.)

Beverages accounted for the largest percentage of sales in these stores (77%); this represented a change from 10 years earlier, when about half of store revenues had come from sales of whole-bean coffees. (See **Exhibit 4** for retail sales mix by product type; see **Exhibit 5** for a typical menu board and price list.)

Starbucks also sold coffee products through non-company-operated retail channels; these so-called "Specialty Operations" accounted for 15% of net revenues. About 27% of these revenues came from North American food-service accounts, that is, sales of whole-bean and ground coffees to hotels, airlines, restaurants, and the like. Another 18% came from domestic retail store licenses that, in

---

[3] Batsell.

[4] Starbucks had recently begun experimenting with drive-throughs. Less than 10% of its stores had drive-throughs, but in these stores, the drive-throughs accounted for 50% of all business.

North America, were only granted when there was no other way to achieve access to desirable retail space (e.g., in airports).

The remaining 55% of specialty revenues came from a variety of sources, including international licensed stores, grocery stores and warehouse clubs (Kraft Foods handled marketing and distribution for Starbucks in this channel), and online and mail-order sales. Starbucks also had a joint venture with Pepsi-Cola to distribute bottled Frappuccino beverages in North America, as well as a partnership with Dreyer's Grand Ice Cream to develop and distribute a line of premium ice creams.

Day explained the company's broad distribution strategy:

> Our philosophy is pretty straightforward—we want to reach customers where they work, travel, shop, and dine. In order to do this, we sometimes have to establish relationships with third parties that share our values and commitment to quality. This is a particularly effective way to reach newcomers with our brand. It's a lot less intimidating to buy Starbucks at a grocery store than it is to walk into one of our coffeehouses for the first time. In fact, about 40% of our new coffeehouse customers have already tried the Starbucks brand before they walk through our doors. Even something like ice cream has become an important trial vehicle for us.

Starbucks Partners

All Starbucks employees were called "partners." The company employed 60,000 partners worldwide, about 50,000 in North America. Most were hourly-wage employees (called *baristas*) who worked in Starbucks retail stores. Alling remarked, "From day one, Howard has made clear his belief that partner satisfaction leads to customer satisfaction. This belief is part of Howard's DNA, and because it's been pounded into each and every one of us, it's become part of our DNA too."

The company had a generous policy of giving health insurance and stock options to even the most entry-level partners, most of whom were between the ages of 17 and 23. Partly as a result of this, Starbucks' partner satisfaction rate consistently hovered in the 80% to 90% range, well above the industry norm,[5] and the company had recently been ranked 47th in the *Fortune* magazine list of best places to work, quite an accomplishment for a company with so many hourly-wage workers.

In addition, Starbucks had one of the lowest employee turnover rates in the industry—just 70%, compared with fast-food industry averages as high as 300%. The rate was even lower for managers, and as Alling noted, the company was always looking for ways to bring turnover down further: "Whenever we have a problem store, we almost always find either an inexperienced store manager or inexperienced baristas. Manager stability is key—it not only decreases partner turnover, but it also enables the store to do a much better job of recognizing regular customers and providing personalized service. So our goal is to make the position a lifetime job."

To this end, the company encouraged promotion from within its own ranks. About 70% of the company's store managers were ex-baristas, and about 60% of its district managers were ex-store managers. In fact, upon being hired, all senior executives had to train and succeed as baristas before being allowed to assume their positions in corporate headquarters.

---

[5] Industrywide, employee satisfaction rates tended to be in the 50% to 60% range. Source: Starbucks, 2000.

Delivering on Service

When a partner was hired to work in one of Starbucks' North American retail stores, he or she had to undergo two types of training. The first type focused on "hard skills" such as learning how to use the cash register and learning how to mix drinks. Most Starbucks beverages were handcrafted, and to ensure product quality, there was a prespecified process associated with each drink. Making an espresso beverage, for example, required seven specific steps.

The other type of training focused on "soft skills." Alling explained:

In our training manual, we explicitly teach partners to connect with customers—to enthusiastically welcome them to the store, to establish eye contact, to smile, and to try to remember their names and orders if they're regulars. We also encourage partners to create conversations with customers using questions that require more than a yes or no answer. So for example, "I noticed you were looking at the menu board—what types of beverages do you typically enjoy?" is a good question for a partner to ask.

Starbucks' "Just Say Yes" policy empowered partners to provide the best service possible, even if it required going beyond company rules. "This means that if a customer spills a drink and asks for a refill, we'll give it to him," said Day. "Or if a customer doesn't have cash and wants to pay with a check (which we aren't supposed to accept), then we'll give her a sample drink for free. The last thing we want to do is win the argument and lose the customer."

Most barista turnover occurred within the first 90 days of employment; if a barista lasted beyond that, there was a high probability that he or she would stay for three years or more. "Our training ends up being a self-selection process," Alling said. Indeed, the ability to balance hard and soft skills required a particular type of person, and Alling believed the challenges had only grown over time:

Back in the days when we sold mostly beans, every customer who walked in the door was a coffee connoisseur, and it was easy for baristas to engage in chitchat while ringing up a bag. Those days are long gone. Today, almost every customer orders a handcrafted beverage. If the line is stretching out the door and everyone's clamoring for their coffee fix, it's not that easy to strike up a conversation with a customer.

The complexity of the barista's job had also increased over time; making a *venti tazoberry and crème*, for instance, required 10 different steps. "It used to be that a barista could make every variation of drink we offered in half a day," Day observed. "Nowadays, given our product proliferation, it would take 16 days of eight-hour shifts. There are literally hundreds of combinations of drinks in our portfolio."

This job complexity was compounded by the fact that almost half of Starbucks' customers customized their drinks. According to Day, this created a tension between product quality and customer focus for Starbucks:

On the one hand, we train baristas to make beverages to our preestablished quality standards—this means enforcing a consistent process that baristas can master. On the other hand, if a customer comes in and wants it their way—extra vanilla, for instance—what should we do? Our heaviest users are always the most demanding. Of course, every time we customize, we slow down the service for everyone else. We also put a lot of strain on our baristas, who are already dealing with an extraordinary number of sophisticated drinks.

One obvious solution to the problem was to hire more baristas to share the workload; however, the company had been extremely reluctant to do this in recent years, particularly given the economic downturn. Labor was already the company's largest expense item in North America (see **Exhibit 3**), and Starbucks stores tended to be located in urban areas with high wage rates. Instead, the company had focused on increasing barista efficiency by removing all non-value-added tasks, simplifying the beverage production process, and tinkering with the facility design to eliminate bottlenecks.

In addition, the company had recently begun installing automated espresso machines in its North American cafés. The *verismo* machines, which decreased the number of steps required to make an espresso beverage, reduced waste, improved consistency, and had generated an overwhelmingly positive customer and barista response.

Measuring Service Performance

Starbucks tracked service performance using a variety of metrics, including monthly status reports and self-reported checklists. The company's most prominent measurement tool was a mystery shopper program called the "Customer Snapshot." Under this program, every store was visited by an anonymous mystery shopper three times a quarter. Upon completing the visit, the shopper would rate the store on four "Basic Service" criteria:

- **Service**—Did the register partner verbally greet the customer? Did the barista and register partner make eye contact with the customer? Say thank you?

- **Cleanliness**—Was the store clean? The counters? The tables? The restrooms?

- **Product quality**—Was the order filled accurately? Was the temperature of the drink within range? Was the beverage properly presented?

- **Speed of service**—How long did the customer have to wait? The company's goal was to serve a customer within three minutes, from back-of-the-line to drink-in-hand. This benchmark was based on market research which indicated that the three-minute standard was a key component in how current Starbucks customers defined "excellent service."

In addition to Basic Service, stores were also rated on "Legendary Service," which was defined as "behavior that created a memorable experience for a customer, that inspired a customer to return often and tell a friend." Legendary Service scores were based on secret shopper observations of service attributes such as partners initiating conversations with customers, partners recognizing customers by name or drink order, and partners being responsive to service problems.

During 2002, the company's Customer Snapshot scores had increased across all stores (see **Exhibit 7**), leading Day to comment, "The Snapshot is not a perfect measurement tool, but we believe it does a good job of measuring trends over the course of a quarter. In order for a store to do well on the Snapshot, it needs to have sustainable processes in place that create a well-established pattern of doing things right so that it gets 'caught' doing things right."

Competition

In the United States, Starbucks competed against a variety of small-scale specialty coffee chains, most of which were regionally concentrated. Each tried to differentiate itself from Starbucks in a different way. For example, Minneapolis-based Caribou Coffee, which operated more than 200 stores in nine states, differentiated itself on store environment. Rather than offer an upscale, pseudo-European atmosphere, its strategy was to simulate the look and feel of an Alaskan lodge, with knotty-

Starbucks: Delivering Customer Service

pine cabinetry, fireplaces, and soft seating. Another example was California-based Peet's Coffee & Tea, which operated about 70 stores in five states. More than 60% of Peet's revenues came from the sale of whole beans. Peet's strategy was to build a super-premium brand by offering the freshest coffee on the market. One of the ways it delivered on this promise was by "roasting to order," that is, by hand roasting small batches of coffee at its California plant and making sure that all of its coffee shipped within 24 hours of roasting.

Starbucks also competed against thousands of independent specialty coffee shops. Some of these independent coffee shops offered a wide range of food and beverages, including beer, wine, and liquor; others offered satellite televisions or Internet-connected computers. Still others differentiated themselves by delivering highly personalized service to an eclectic clientele.

Finally, Starbucks competed against donut and bagel chains such as Dunkin Donuts, which operated over 3,700 stores in 38 states. Dunkin Donuts attributed half of its sales to coffee and in recent years had begun offering flavored coffee and noncoffee alternatives, such as Dunkaccino (a coffee and chocolate combination available with various toppings) and Vanilla Chai (a combination of tea, vanilla, honey, and spices).

Caffeinating the World

The company's overall objective was to establish Starbucks as the "most recognized and respected brand in the world."[6] This ambitious goal required an aggressive growth strategy, and in 2002, the two biggest drivers of company growth were retail expansion and product innovation.

Retail Expansion

Starbucks already owned close to one-third of America's coffee bars, more than its next five biggest competitors combined. (By comparison, the U.S.'s second-largest player, Diedrich Coffee, operated fewer than 400 stores.) However, the company had plans to open 525 company-operated and 225 licensed North American stores in 2003, and Schultz believed that there was no reason North America could not eventually expand to at least 10,000 stores. As he put it, "These are still the early days of the company's growth."[7]

The company's optimistic growth plans were based on a number of considerations:

- First, coffee consumption was on the rise in the United States, following years of decline. More than 109 million people (about half of the U.S. population) now drank coffee every day, and an additional 52 million drank it on occasion. The market's biggest growth appeared to be among drinkers of specialty coffee,[8] and it was estimated that about one-third of all U.S. coffee consumption took place outside of the home, in places such as offices, restaurants, and coffee shops. (See **Exhibit 6**.)

---

[6] Starbucks 2002 Annual Report.

[7] Dina ElBoghdady, "Pouring It On: The Starbucks Strategy? Locations, Locations, Locations," *The Washington Post*, August 25, 2002.

[8] National Coffee Association.

- Second, there were still eight states in the United States without a single company-operated Starbucks; in fact, the company was only in 150 of the roughly 300 metropolitan statistical areas in the nation.

- Third, the company believed it was far from reaching saturation levels in many existing markets. In the Southeast, for example, there was only one store for every 110,000 people (compared with one store for every 20,000 people in the Pacific Northwest). More generally, only seven states had more than 100 Starbucks locations.

Starbucks' strategy for expanding its retail business was to open stores in new markets while geographically clustering stores in existing markets. Although the latter often resulted in significant cannibalization, the company believed that this was more than offset by the total incremental sales associated with the increased store concentration. As Schultz readily conceded, "We self-cannibalize at least a third of our stores every day."[9]

When it came to selecting new retail sites, the company considered a number of criteria, including the extent to which the demographics of the area matched the profile of the typical Starbucks drinker, the level of coffee consumption in the area, the nature and intensity of competition in the local market, and the availability of attractive real estate. Once a decision was made to move forward with a site, the company was capable of designing, permitting, constructing, and opening a new store within 16 weeks. A new store typically averaged about $610,000 in sales during its first year; same-store sales (comps) were strongest in the first three years and then continued to comp positively, consistent with the company average.

Starbucks' international expansion plans were equally ambitious. Starbucks already operated over 300 company-owned stores in the United Kingdom, Australia, and Thailand, in addition to about 900 licensed stores in various countries in Asia, Europe, the Middle East, Africa, and Latin America. (Its largest international market was Japan, with close to 400 stores.) The company's goal was to ultimately have 15,000 international stores.

Product Innovation

The second big driver of company growth was product innovation. Internally, this was considered one of the most significant factors in comparable store sales growth, particularly since Starbucks' prices had remained relatively stable in recent years. New products were launched on a regular basis; for example, Starbucks introduced at least one new hot beverage every holiday season.

The new product development process generally operated on a 12- to 18-month cycle, during which the internal research and development (R&D) team tinkered with product formulations, ran focus groups, and conducted in-store experiments and market tests. Aside from consumer acceptance, whether a product made it to market depended on a number of factors, including the extent to which the drink fit into the "ergonomic flow" of operations and the speed with which the beverage could be handcrafted. Most importantly, the success of a new beverage depended on partner acceptance. "We've learned that no matter how great a drink it is, if our partners aren't excited about it, it won't sell," said Alling.

In recent years, the company's most successful innovation had been the 1995 introduction of a coffee and non-coffee-based line of Frappuccino beverages, which had driven same-store sales primarily by boosting traffic during nonpeak hours. The bottled version of the beverage (distributed

---

[9] ElBoghdady.

by PepsiCo) had become a $400 million[10] franchise; it had managed to capture 90% of the ready-to-drink coffee category, in large part due to its appeal to non-coffee-drinking 20-somethings.

Service Innovation

In terms of nonproduct innovation, Starbucks' stored-value card (SVC) had been launched in November 2001. This prepaid, swipeable smart card—which Schultz referred to as "the most significant product introduction since Frappuccino"[11]—could be used to pay for transactions in any company-operated store in North America. Early indications of the SVC's appeal were very positive: After less than one year on the market, about 6 million cards had been issued, and initial activations and reloads had already reached $160 million in sales. In surveys, the company had learned that cardholders tended to visit Starbucks twice as often as cash customers and tended to experience reduced transaction times.

Day remarked, "We've found that a lot of the cards are being given away as gifts, and many of those gift recipients are being introduced to our brand for the first time. Not to mention the fact that the cards allow us to collect all kinds of customer-transaction data, data that we haven't even begun to do anything with yet."

The company's latest service innovation was its T-Mobile HotSpot wireless Internet service, introduced in August 2002. The service offered high-speed access to the Internet in selected Starbucks stores in the United States and Europe, starting at $49.99 a month.

Starbucks' Market Research: Trouble Brewing?

Interestingly, although Starbucks was considered one of the world's most effective marketing organizations, it lacked a strategic marketing group. In fact, the company had no chief marketing officer, and its marketing department functioned as three separate groups—a market research group that gathered and analyzed market data requested by the various business units, a category group that developed new products and managed the menu and margins, and a marketing group that developed the quarterly promotional plans.

This organizational structure forced all of Starbucks' senior executives to assume marketing-related responsibilities. As Day pointed out, "Marketing is everywhere at Starbucks—it just doesn't necessarily show up in a line item called 'marketing.' Everyone has to get involved in a collaborative marketing effort." However, the organizational structure also meant that market- and customer-related trends could sometimes be overlooked. "We tend to be great at measuring things, at collecting market data," Day noted, "but we are not very disciplined when it comes to using this data to drive decision making." She continued:

> This is exactly what started to happen a few years ago. We had evidence coming in from market research that contradicted some of the fundamental assumptions we had about our brand and our customers. The problem was that this evidence was all over the place—no one was really looking at the "big picture." As a result, it took awhile before we started to take notice.

---

[10] Refers to sales at retail. Actual revenue contribution was much lower due to the joint-venture structure.

[11] Stanley Holmes, "Starbucks' Card Smarts," *BusinessWeek*, March 18, 2002.

Starbucks' Brand Meaning

Once the team did take notice, it discovered several things. First, despite Starbucks' overwhelming presence and convenience, there was very little image or product differentiation between Starbucks and the smaller coffee chains (other than Starbucks' ubiquity) in the minds of specialty coffeehouse customers. There *was* significant differentiation, however, between Starbucks and the independent specialty coffeehouses (see **Table A** below).

Table A   Qualitative Brand Meaning: Independents vs. Starbucks

Independents:
- Social and inclusive
- Diverse and intellectual
- Artsy and funky
- Liberal and free-spirited
- Lingering encouraged
- Particularly appealing to younger coffeehouse customers
- Somewhat intimidating to older, more mainstream coffeehouse customers

Starbucks:
- Everywhere—the trend
- Good coffee on the run
- Place to meet and move on
- Convenience oriented; on the way to work
- Accessible and consistent

Source: Starbucks, based on qualitative interviews with specialty-coffeehouse customers.

More generally, the market research team discovered that Starbucks' brand image had some rough edges. The number of respondents who strongly agreed with the statement "Starbucks cares primarily about making money" was up from 53% in 2000 to 61% in 2001, while the number of respondents who strongly agreed with the statement "Starbucks cares primarily about building more stores" was up from 48% to 55%. Day noted, "It's become apparent that we need to ask ourselves, 'Are we focusing on the right things? Are we clearly communicating our value and values to our customers, instead of just our growth plans?'" (see **Table B** below).

Table B   The Top Five Attributes Consumers Associate with the Starbucks Brand

- Known for specialty/gourmet coffee (54% strongly agree)
- Widely available (43% strongly agree)
- Corporate (42% strongly agree)
- Trendy (41% strongly agree)
- Always feel welcome at Starbucks (39% strongly agree)

Source: Starbucks, based on 2002 survey.

The Changing Customer

The market research team also discovered that Starbucks' customer base was evolving. Starbucks' newer customers tended to be younger, less well-educated, and in a lower income bracket than Starbucks' more established customers. In addition, they visited the stores less frequently and had very different perceptions of the Starbucks brand compared to more established customers (see **Exhibit 8**).

Furthermore, the team learned that Starbucks' historical customer profile—the affluent, well-educated, white-collar female between the ages of 24 and 44—had expanded. For example, about half of the stores in southern California had large numbers of Hispanic customers. In Florida, the company had stores that catered primarily to Cuban-Americans.

Customer Behavior

With respect to customer behavior, the market research team discovered that, regardless of the market—urban versus rural, new versus established—customers tended to use the stores the same way. The team also learned that, although the company's most frequent customers averaged 18 visits a month, the typical customer visited just five times a month (see **Figure A** below).

Figure A   Customer Visit Frequency

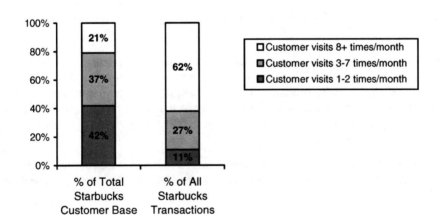

Source: Starbucks, 2002.

Measuring and Driving Customer Satisfaction

Finally, the team discovered that, despite its high Customer Snapshot scores, Starbucks was not meeting expectations in terms of customer satisfaction. The satisfaction scores were considered critical because the team also had evidence of a direct link between satisfaction level and customer loyalty (see **Exhibit 9** for customer satisfaction data).

While customer satisfaction was driven by a number of different factors (see **Exhibit 10**), Day believed that the customer satisfaction gap could primarily be attributed to a *service gap* between Starbucks scores on key attributes and customer expectations. When Starbucks had polled its customers to determine what it could do to make them feel more like valued customers, "improvements to service"—in particular, speed-of-service—had been mentioned most frequently (see **Exhibit 11** for more information).

Rediscovering the Starbucks Customer

Responding to the market research findings posed a difficult management challenge. The most controversial proposal was the one on the table before Day—it involved relaxing the labor-hour controls in the stores to add an additional 20 hours of labor, per week, per store, at a cost of an extra $40 million per year. Not surprisingly, the plan was being met with significant internal resistance. "Our CFO is understandably concerned about the potential impact on our bottom line," said Day. "Each $6 million in profit contribution translates into a penny a share. But my argument is that if we move away from seeing labor as an expense to seeing it as a customer-oriented investment, we'll see a positive return." She continued:

> We need to bring service time down to the three-minute level in all of our stores, regardless of the time of day. If we do this, we'll not only increase customer satisfaction and build stronger long-term relationships with our customers, we'll also improve our customer throughput. The goal is to move each store closer to the $20,000 level in terms of weekly sales, and I think that this plan will help us get there.

In two days, Day was scheduled to make a final recommendation to Howard Schultz and Orin Smith about whether the company should roll out the $40 million plan. In preparation for this meeting, Day had asked Alling to help her think through the implications of the plan one final time. She mused:

> We've been operating with the assumption that we do customer service well. But the reality is, we've started to lose sight of the consumer. It's amazing that this could happen to a company like us—after all, we've become one of the most prominent consumer brands in the world. For all of our focus on building the brand and introducing new products, we've simply stopped talking about the customer. We've lost the connection between satisfying our customers and growing the business.

Alling's response was simple: "We know that both Howard and Orin are totally committed to satisfying our retail customers. Our challenge is to tie customer satisfaction to the bottom line. What evidence do we have?"

Starbucks: Delivering Customer Service

Exhibit 1   Starbucks' Financials, FY 1998 to FY 2002 ($ in millions)

	FY 1998	FY 1999	FY 2000	FY 2001	FY 2002
Revenue					
Co-Owned North American	1,076.8	1,375.0	1,734.9	2,086.4	2,583.8
Co-Owned Int'l (UK, Thailand, Australia)	25.8	48.4	88.7	143.2	209.1
Total Company-Operated Retail	1,102.6	1,423.4	1,823.6	2,229.6	2,792.9
Specialty Operations	206.1	263.4	354.0	419.4	496.0
Net Revenues	**1,308.7**	**1,686.8**	**2,177.6**	**2,649.0**	**3,288.9**
Cost of Goods Sold	578.5	747.6	961.9	1,112.8	1,350.0
Gross Profit	**730.2**	**939.2**	**1,215.7**	**1,536.2**	**1,938.9**
Joint-Venture Income[a]	1.0	3.2	20.3	28.6	35.8
Expenses:					
Store Operating Expense	418.5	543.6	704.9	875.5	1,121.1
Other Operating Expense	44.5	54.6	78.4	93.3	127.2
Depreciation & Amortization Expense	72.5	97.8	130.2	163.5	205.6
General & Admin Expense	77.6	89.7	110.2	151.4	202.1
Operating Expenses	**613.1**	**785.7**	**1,023.8**	**1,283.7**	**1,656.0**
Operating Profit	**109.2**	**156.7**	**212.3**	**281.1**	**310.0**
Net Income	**68.4**	**101.7**	**94.5**	**181.2**	**215.1**
% Change in Monthly Comparable Store Sales[b]					
North America	5%	6%	9%	5%	7%
Consolidated	5%	6%	9%	5%	6%

Source: Adapted from company reports and Lehman Brothers, November 5, 2002.

[a]Includes income from various joint ventures, including Starbucks' partnership with the Pepsi-Cola Company to develop and distribute Frappuccino and with Dreyer's Grand Ice Cream to develop and distribute premium ice creams.

[b]Includes only company-operated stores open 13 months or longer.

Exhibit 2   Starbucks' Store Growth

	FY 1998	FY 1999	FY 2000	FY 2001	FY 2002
Total North America	**1,755**	**2,217**	**2,976**	**3,780**	**4,574**
Company-Operated	1,622	2,038	2,446	2,971	3,496
Licensed Stores[a]	133	179	530	809	1,078
Total International	**131**	**281**	**525**	**929**	**1,312**
Company-Operated	66	97	173	295	384
Licensed Stores	65	184	352	634	928
Total Stores	**1,886**	**2,498**	**3,501**	**4,709**	**5,886**

Source: Company reports.

[a]Includes kiosks located in grocery stores, bookstores, hotels, airports, and so on.

Exhibit 3   Additional Data, North American Company-Operated Stores (FY2002)

	Average
Average hourly rate with shift supervisors and hourly partners	$ 9.00
Total labor hours per week, average store	360
Average weekly store volume	$15,400
Average ticket	$ 3.85
Average daily customer count, per store	570

Source: Company reports.

Exhibit 4   Product Mix, North American Company-Operated Stores (FY2002)

	Percent of Sales
Retail Product Mix	
Coffee Beverages	77%
Food Items	13%
Whole-Bean Coffees	6%
Equipment & Accessories	4%

Source: Company reports.

Starbucks: Delivering Customer Service   504-016

Exhibit 5   Typical Menu Board and Price List for North American Company-Owned Store

Espresso Traditions	Tall	Grande	Venti
Classic Favorites			
Toffee Nut Latte	2.95	3.50	3.80
Vanilla Latte	2.85	3.40	3.70
Caffe Latte	2.55	3.10	3.40
Cappuccino	2.55	3.10	3.40
Caramel Macchiato	2.80	3.40	3.65
White Chocolate Mocha	3.20	3.75	4.00
Caffe Mocha	2.75	3.30	3.55
Caffe Americano	1.75	2.05	2.40

Espresso	Solo		Doppio
Espresso	1.45		1.75

Extras		
Additional Espresso Shot		.55
Add flavored syrup		.30
Organic milk & soy available upon request		

Frappuccino	Tall	Grande	Venti
Ice Blended Beverages			
Coffee	2.65	3.15	3.65
Mocha	2.90	3.40	3.90
Caramel Frappuccino	3.15	3.65	4.15
Mocha Coconut	3.15	3.65	4.15
(limited offering)			

Crème Frappuccino	Tall	Grande	Venti
Ice Blended Crème			
Toffee Nut Crème	3.15	3.65	4.15
Vanilla Crème	2.65	3.15	3.65
Coconut Crème	3.15	3.65	4.15

Tazo Tea Frappuccino	Tall	Grande	Venti
Ice Blended Teas			
Tazo Citrus	2.90	3.40	3.90
Tazoberry	2.90	3.40	3.90
Tazo Chai Crème	3.15	3.65	4.15

Brewed Coffee	Tall	Grande	Venti
Coffee of the Day	1.40	1.60	1.70
Decaf of the Day	1.40	1.60	1.70

Cold Beverages	Tall	Grande	Venti
Iced Caffe Latte	2.55	3.10	3.50
Iced Caramel Macchiato	2.80	3.40	3.80
Iced Caffe Americano	1.75	2.05	3.40

Coffee Alternatives	Tall	Grande	Venti
Toffee Nut Crème	2.45	2.70	2.95
Vanilla Crème	2.20	2.45	2.70
Caramel Apple Cider	2.45	2.70	2.95
Hot Chocolate	2.20	2.45	2.70
Tazo Hot Tea	1.15	1.65	1.65
Tazo Chai	2.70	3.10	3.35

Whole Beans: Bold	½ lb	1 lb
Our most intriguing and exotic coffees		
Gold Coast Blend	5.70	10.95
French Roast	5.20	9.95
Sumatra	5.30	10.15
Decaf Sumatra	5.60	10.65
Ethiopia Sidame	5.20	9.95
Arabian Mocha Sanani	8.30	15.95
Kenya	5.30	10.15
Italian Roast	5.20	9.95
Sulawesi	6.10	11.65

Whole Beans: Smooth	½ lb	1 lb
Richer, more flavorful coffees		
Espresso Roast	5.20	9.95
Decaf Espresso Roast	5.60	10.65
Yukon Blend	5.20	9.95
Café Verona	5.20	9.95
Guatemala Antigua	5.30	10.15
Arabian Mocha Java	6.30	11.95
Decaf Mocha Java/SWP	6.50	12.45

Whole Beans: Mild	½ lb	1 lb
The perfect introduction to Starbucks coffees		
Breakfast Blend	5.20	9.95
Lightnote Blend	5.20	9.95
Decaf Lightnote Blend	5.60	10.65
Colombia Narino	5.50	10.45
House Blend	5.20	9.95
Decaf House Blend	5.60	10.65
Fair Trade Coffee	5.95	11.45

Source: Starbucks location: Harvard Square, Cambridge, Massachusetts, February 2003.

Exhibit 6   Total U.S. Retail Coffee Market (includes both in-home and out-of-home consumption)

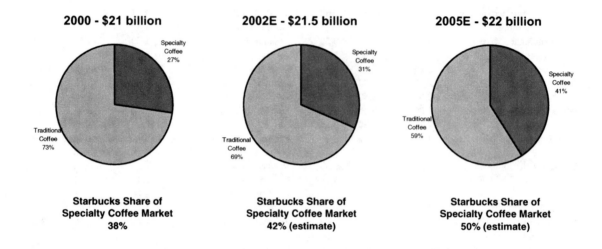

Other estimates[a] for the U.S. retail coffee market in 2002:

- In the home, specialty coffee[b] was estimated to be a $3.2 billion business, of which Starbucks was estimated to have a 4% share.

- In the food-service channel, specialty coffee was estimated to be a $5 billion business, of which Starbucks was estimated to have a 5% share.

- In grocery stores, Starbucks was estimated to have a 7.3% share in the ground-coffee category and a 21.7% share in the whole-beans category.

- It was estimated that over the next several years, the overall retail market would grow less than 1% per annum, but growth in the specialty-coffee category would be strong, with compound annual growth rate (CAGR) of 9% to 10%.

- Starbucks' U.S. business was projected to grow at a CAGR of approximately 20% top-line revenue growth.

Source: Adapted from company reports and Lehman Brothers, November 5, 2002.

[a]The value of the retail coffee market was difficult to estimate given the highly fragmented and loosely monitored nature of the market (i.e., specialty coffeehouses, restaurants, delis, kiosks, street carts, grocery and convenience stores, vending machines, etc.).

[b]Specialty coffee includes espresso, cappuccino, latte, café mocha, iced/ice-blended coffee, gourmet coffee (premium whole bean or ground), and blended coffee.

Starbucks: Delivering Customer Service   504-016

Exhibit 7   Customer Snapshot Scores (North American stores)

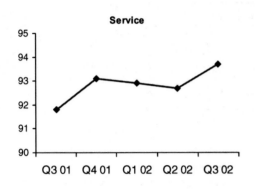
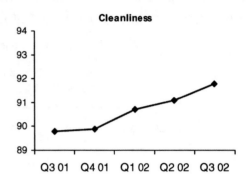

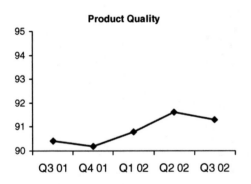
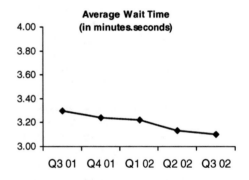

Source: Company information.

504-016   Starbucks: Delivering Customer Service

Exhibit 8   Starbucks' Customer Retention Information

% of Starbucks' customers who first started visiting Starbucks . . .	
In the past year	27%
1–2 years ago	20%
2–5 years ago	30%
5 or more years ago	23%

Source: Starbucks, 2002. Based on a sample of Starbucks' 2002 customer base.

	New Customers (first visited in past year)	Established Customers (first visited 5+ years ago)
Percent female	45%	49%
Average Age	36	40
Percent with College Degree +	37%	63%
Average income	$65,000	$81,000
Average # cups of coffee/week (includes at home and away from home)	15	19
Attitudes toward Starbucks:		
High-quality brand	34%	51%
Brand I trust	30%	50%
For someone like me	15%	40%
Worth paying more for	8%	32%
Known for specialty coffee	44%	60%
Known as the coffee expert	31%	45%
Best-tasting coffee	20%	31%
Highest-quality coffee	26%	41%
Overall opinion of Starbucks	**25%**	**44%**

Source: Starbucks, 2002. "Attitudes toward Starbucks" measured according to the percent of customers who agreed with the above statements.

Exhibit 9   Starbucks' Customer Behavior, by Satisfaction Level

	Unsatisfied Customer	Satisfied Customer	Highly Satisfied Customer
Number of Starbucks Visits/Month	3.9	4.3	7.2
Average Ticket Size/Visit	$3.88	$4.06	$4.42
Average Customer Life (Years)	1.1	4.4	8.3

Source: Self-reported customer activity from Starbucks survey, 2002.

Starbucks: Delivering Customer Service

Exhibit 10 Importance Rankings of Key Attributes in Creating Customer Satisfaction

To be read: *83% of Starbucks' customers rate a clean store as being highly important (90+ on a 100-point scale) in creating customer satisfaction.*

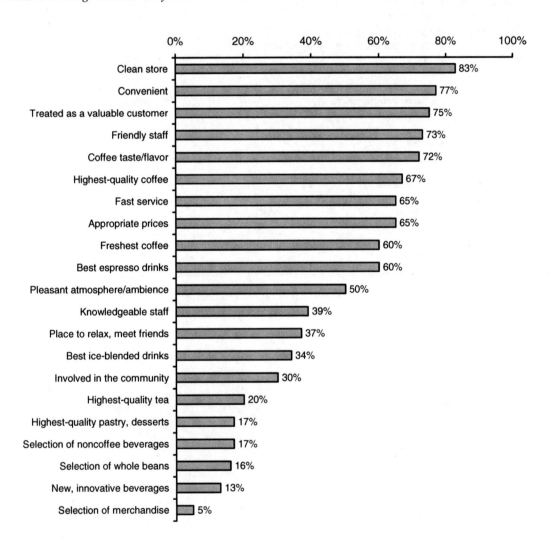

Source: Self-reported customer activity from Starbucks survey, 2002.

504-016

Exhibit 11 Factors Driving "Valued Customer" Perceptions

How could Starbucks make you feel more like a valued customer?	% Responses
Improvements to Service (total)	**34%**
Friendlier, more attentive staff	19%
Faster, more efficient service	10%
Personal treatment (remember my name, remember my order)	4%
More knowledgeable staff	4%
Better service	2%
Offer Better Prices/Incentive Programs (total)	**31%**
Free cup after x number of visits	19%
Reduce prices	11%
Offer promotions, specials	3%
Other (total)	**21%**
Better quality/Variety of products	9%
Improve atmosphere	8%
Community outreach/Charity	2%
More stores/More convenient locations	2%
Don't Know/Already Satisfied	**28%**

Source: Starbucks, 2002. Based on a survey of Starbucks' 2002 customer base, including highly satisfied, satisfied, and unsatisfied customers.

Harvard Business School

9-595-057

Rev. March 30, 2001

The Black & Decker Corporation (A): Power Tools Division

Joe, I like you guys. But, look, I give Makita 10 feet of space. I give you 10 feet of space. They outsell you 8 to 1. What are we going to do about that?

In January 1991, statements like this no longer surprise Joseph Galli. Black & Decker's (B&D) vice president of sales and marketing for power tools had heard similar sentiments expressed by many trade accounts. Makita Electric of Japan had practically taken over the professional power tools for tradesmen business since it entered the United States market a decade ago. "Tradesmen" was one of the three major segments of the power tools business—the others being "Consumer" and "Industrial." "Consumer" represented "at home" use, while both "Tradesmen" and "Industrial" covered professional users. The distinguishing characteristic of the Tradesmen segment was that these buyers, such as a carpenter, bought tools for their own use on a job site. In Industrial, the buyer was generally a corporation purchasing tools for use by employees. By late 1990, Makita's success in the Professional-Tradesmen segment was such that it held an 80% share in cordless drills, the single largest product category, and a 50% segment share overall. B&D had virtually created the portable power tools business in the United States beginning in the early 1900s. While it maintained the #1 market share position in the Consumer and Professional-Industrial segments, its entry in the relatively new Professional-Tradesmen segment held only about a 9% share.

The trade was asking for advertising allowances and rebate money on B&D's Tradesmen products and profitability in this segment was near zero. B&D's senior management resolved to put an end to this "no win" game, and Galli set about developing and gaining corporate support for a viable program to challenge Makita for leadership in this segment. He could not help but see the irony of a 9% Tradesmen segment share and no profitability against the results of two recent research studies: one showing B&D to be among the powerful brand names in the world, and the second establishing B&D's professional tools to be the highest quality in the industry.

Black & Decker

In 1910, Duncan Black and Alonzo Decker, Sr., started a machine shop and, in 1917, received a patent on the world's first portable power drill with pistol grip and trigger switch; 73 years after receiving its first patent, B&D was the world's largest producer of power tools, power tool accessories, electric lawn and garden tools, and residential security hardware. Headquartered in

Towson, Maryland, B&D's sales reached $4.8 billion in 1990, with nearly 50% of product revenues from outside the United States. Alonzo G. Decker, Jr., was honorary chairman of the company and a member of the board of directors. He had been chairman of the board and chief executive officer from 1968 to 1975. Prior to his becoming CEO, the CEO post had always been held by his father or co-founder Black. From its roots in power tools, B&D began a move "from the garage to the house" in 1979 with the introduction of the very successful Dustbuster® hand-held vacuum. This "into the house" thrust led to the purchase of General Electric's Housewares Division in 1984 for $212 million. As part of the sale agreement, B&D could use General Electric's name on products only until 1987.

Nolan Archibald, a Harvard Business School graduate and a former group president at Beatrice, became president and CEO in 1986. The early 1980s had been volatile years at B&D. It began the decade with a 19% net revenue increase to $1.2 billion in 1980, but sales stagnated at this level through 1983. In 1985, with net revenues at $1.7 billion, B&D posted a $215.1 million restructuring cost and a $158.4 million loss. For the 5-year period from 1981 through 1985, the company lost money. B&D's $2.8 billion acquisition of Emhart Corporation in 1989 more than doubled B&D's revenues and brought new strong brands, including Kwikset® locks and Price Pfister® faucets, but raised the company's long-term debt to $4.2 billion, representing about 84% of total capital. **Figure A** shows the growth in B&D sales and net income since Archibald became CEO.

Figure A Black & Decker Revenues and Operating Income, 1986-1990

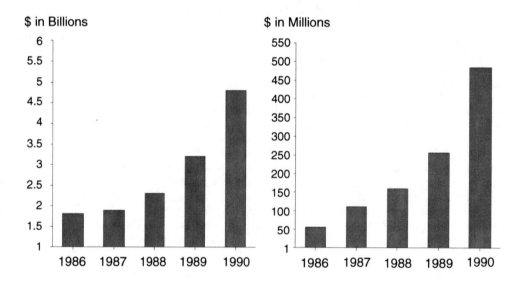

The five largest product groups and their percentage of B&D's 1990 sales were:

• Power Tools and Accessories	29%
• Household Products	15%
• Information Systems and Services	11%
• Outdoor Products	9%
• Security Hardware	9%

Household products included hand-held vacuums, irons, mixers, food processors and choppers, coffee makers, and toasters and toaster ovens. The well-known Dustbuster and Spacemaker® (under-the-cabinet appliances) brands were part of this group. The B&D franchise was especially strong in cordless vacuums, irons, and toaster ovens, each holding over a 50% market share in the United States. In 1990, 29 new household products were introduced, including the Power Pro™ Dustbuster® heavy duty cordless vacuum. The household products line was heavily supported with media advertising.

The B&D name enjoyed substantial equity in both the United States and Europe. An independent survey of 6,000 brands showed Black & Decker's brand-strength ranking to be #7 in the United States and #19 in Europe.[1] This put Black & Decker in the company of Coca-Cola, Campbell's, Walt Disney, Pepsi-Cola, Kodak, NBC, Kellogg's, McDonald's, and Hershey—the other firms rounding out the U.S. top ten.

Power Tools Market

In 1990, portable power tools in the United States was a $1.5 billion market. Products ranged from an electric screwdriver for the consumer who might use it once a year at home to heavy-duty miter saws used continually throughout the day at construction sites. Segmentation of the market was as shown in **Figure B**.

Figure B   Segmentation of the U.S. Power Tools Market

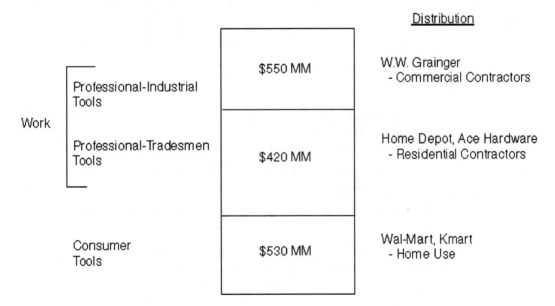

Nonprofessional users accounted for $530 million or 35% of the market. In this Consumer segment, consumers bought tools at mass merchants, such as Wal-Mart and Kmart, and hardware stores for their own home use. The "for work" market was divided into a Professional-Industrial segment and a Professional-Tradesmen segment. The $550 million Professional-Industrial segment was made up primarily of commercial contractors working on large projects (e.g., office buildings,

---

[1]Landor Associates Survey.

bridges, etc.) and company assembly lines (e.g., automobile plants). In this segment, distributors (of which W.W. Grainger of Skokie, Illinois, with over 300 branch offices, was by far the largest) played an important role in providing technical expertise and service. For a given job, the distributor could both specify the contractor's tool requirements and recommend specific brands. Grainger stocked more than 32,000 items to provide prompt delivery. In the Professional-Industrial segment, tools were typically purchased and owned by the company rather than the individual users.

The Professional-Tradesmen segment was targeted largely at tradesmen such as electricians, plumbers, carpenters, framers, roofers, and general remodelers working in residential construction. These tradespeople were expected to show up at the job site with their own necessary tools of the trade in working condition. These buyers tended to patronize newly emerging retail distribution channels including home centers such as The Home Depot and Lowe's, in addition to the traditional hardware stores, such as Ace. While the smallest of the three segments in 1990, at $420 million (28%), Professional-Tradesmen was growing fastest at 9% compared with a 7% growth rate for Consumer and no growth for Professional-Industrial. Some "heavy do-it-yourselfers" bought tools in the Professional-Tradesmen segment, but this segment primarily comprised people who made a living with their tools.

B&D participated in all three segments. Black & Decker®-brand power tools held nearly a 30% share of the U.S. market overall.[2] To serve these segments, B&D offered three separate lines and brand designations all under the Black & Decker family name, as follows:

U.S. Market Segment	Brand Logo	Product Color	Approximate B&D Segment Share 1990	Approximate B&D Segment Revenues 1990
Professional-Industrial • Size = $550MM	BLACK & DECKER Industrial Heavy Duty Power Tools	Charcoal Grey	20%	$110 MM
Professional-Tradesmen • Size = $420MM	BLACK & DECKER Professional Power Tools & Accessories	Charcoal Grey	9%	$35 MM
Consumer • Size = $530MM	BLACK & DECKER.	Black	45%	$250 MM

In the Professional-Industrial segment, B&D's share was near parity with Milwaukee Electric of Brookfield, Wisconsin. Founded in 1924, Milwaukee was a privately held firm, selling only in the high end of the market at a rate of approximately $200 million per year worldwide. The second tier suppliers in the Professional-Industrial segment were Bosch, Porter Cable, and Makita. The very knowledgeable purchase decision influencers in the Professional-Industrial segment viewed B&D as offering high-quality, differentiated products and excellent service. At the other end of the performance spectrum, in the Consumer segment, B&D's brand recognition and image helped it attain the #1 position in the marketplace with nearly a 50% share over suppliers such as Skil, Craftsman, Wen, and various private label products.

---

[2]In addition, it manufactured some professional power tools under the Craftsman label for Sears, which held an additional 4% of the Professional-Tradesmen segment.

The Black & Decker Corporation (A): Power Tools Division 595-057

B&D's strengths in the Professional-Industrial and Consumer segments did not transfer to the Professional-Tradesmen segment, where the approximate share positions in 1990 were as shown in **Table A**.

Table A   Power Tools, Professional-Tradesmen
Approximate Segment Shares, 1990

Makita	~50%
Milwaukee	~10%
Black & Decker	~9%
Ryobi	~9%
Skil	~5%
Craftsman[a]	~5%
Porter-Cable	~3%
Bosch	~3%

[a]Manufactured in part by B&D and marketed by Sears.

Three product types—drills, saws, and sanders—represented nearly 80% of the total sales in the Professional-Tradesmen segment. The top three manufacturers offered broad product lines at approximately 175 SKUs each. Since its entry into the market in 1978, Makita had staked out leadership positions in virtually all products and distribution types within the Professional-Tradesmen segment. **Exhibit 1** shows approximate shares for Makita, Milwaukee, and B&D for the largest categories in the segment. **Exhibit 2** shows shares of Makita and B&D by the five major outlet types: (i) Two-Step (sales through distributors to independent retailers, such as Ace and ServiStar), (ii) Home Centers, (iii) Warehouse Home Centers, (iv) Membership Clubs, and (v) Farm Outlets.

Professional-Tradesmen revenues of approximately $35 million in 1990 for B&D translated into about $3 million in operating income. Gross margins ran about 35%, but SG+A costs were about 25%.

These numbers had become even more vivid for Galli in a recent Monday morning conversation with his boss, Gary DiCamillo, B&D's president of Power Tools for the United States, who recounted this story:

> Joe, yesterday, I stopped by that new Home Depot. It was a nice afternoon; lots of people around. They had one of those woodworking guys out on the sidewalk giving demonstrations for a couple of hours. He was using all Skil saws, and he was just packing up to go home when I came by at about 4 o'clock.
>
> I said to him "What do you think of the Skil saws?" "Pretty good," he said. So, I said, "Who else do you like?" He said "Oh, Milwaukee makes a nice reciprocating saw; Ryobi's got some okay things." "What about Makita?" I said. He said, "Oh, they're okay—they're all pretty good really—you just have to stay away from that Black & Decker!"

Black & Decker and the Professional Segment Buyer

While the "just got to stay away from that Black & Decker" view was perhaps extreme, Galli understood that B&D's strength as a consumer brand was not necessarily beneficial for the Professional-Tradesmen segment. Some tradespeople viewed all B&D products as for use at home rather than on the job; and, conversely, there had been instances of a B&D product designed for at home use being subjected to the demands of the job site and failing.

The typical plumber, electrician, or general remodeler working in residential construction had about $3,000 invested in 10 or so "tools-of-the-trade." He or she bought tools when a replacement was needed, spending on average $1,000 per year. Tools and their performance were a constant topic of conversation at the job site. Generally, tradespeople were satisfied with the tools available—the perception being that Makita provided a good baseline option in all major categories, and other suppliers had particular product strengths, e.g., Skil in circular saws.

As noted above in **Exhibit 2**, this buyer bought most frequently in independently owned stores served by distributors, i.e., the Two-Step in **Exhibit 2**. However, the Home Centers noted in **Exhibit 2** were growing in importance. For example, the largest single outlet of Professional-Tradesmen tool sales in 1990 was The Home Depot at approximately $5 million; second was Home Club at $3.5 million, compared to the largest of the Two-Steps, Ace and ServiStar, at $2 million each. The Home Depot was the largest of the rapidly growing collection of home improvement chain stores. With 145 stores and $3.8 billion in 1990 sales, The Home Depot's strategy was to stock 30,000 items in a 100,000 square foot location, with prices about 30% less than the traditional hardware store, while also providing superior customer service. Makita's rise to marketplace dominance was aided by the rapid development of this new type of distribution.

B&D's research on tradespeople's perceptions of suppliers' quality showed four tiers in the marketplace, as shown in **Figure C**.

Figure C   Brand Perceptions of Professional-Tradesmen Segment Buyers

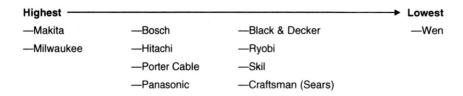

Highest			Lowest
—Makita	—Bosch	—Black & Decker	—Wen
—Milwaukee	—Hitachi	—Ryobi	
	—Porter Cable	—Skil	
	—Panasonic	—Craftsman (Sears)	

Both Milwaukee and Makita priced at premiums over B&D, averaging 10% and 5%, respectively. Despite the price premium over B&D, Makita's prices on some products were less than half of what the product sold for in Makita's home market, Japan, where Makita was #2 in market share to Hitachi.

While Makita's position with tradespeople was strong, retailers were not uniformly positive toward Makita. Some regarded it as "arrogant and dictatorial." Makita offered no channel protection, selling the same products throughout a range of outlets including the discount oriented Membership Clubs, which B&D had decided not to include among its distributors of Professional-Tradesmen tools (see **Exhibit 2**). Some believed Makita to be "trading-down" its offerings by, among other things, positioning them as appropriate for Father's Day giving.

While no tradesperson would explicitly note "product color" as a key attribute in the purchase decision, color was generally regarded as a significant product differentiator. Consumer tool manufacturers had largely followed B&D's 1981 lead of making consumer tools black or charcoal grey. B&D's policy was to use black as its consumer grade color and charcoal grey for its Professional-Industrial and Professional-Tradesmen grades. Competing brands of professional tools were more highly differentiated in color, as shown in **Figure D**.

Figure D   Color Differentiation: Professional End Users

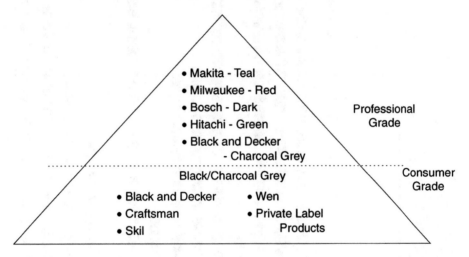

Black & Decker Product Research

Product development had been a B&D focus since 1985 and B&D tools were highly regarded in the demanding Professional-Industrial segment, so Galli believed that the source of B&D's share problem in the Professional-Tradesmen segment was not inherent product quality. This belief was tested in two ways. First, B&D conducted laboratory tests on its own and competitive products to assess performance, reliability, and durability. **Figure E** summarizes the results for the 14 major Professional-Tradesmen products. B&D's offerings were characterized on a scale ranging from weak/undeveloped to competitive to leadership.

Second, B&D did extensive field tests. All identifying marks and colors were removed from products (both B&D and competitors). The products were then used in actual work situations for one month. Users provided comments on product performance and their interest in buying the product when a replacement was needed. This user testing supported the findings of the laboratory tests of **Figure E**, i.e., B&D's product quality was very strongly competitive in the large majority of product categories.

Figure E   Black & Decker Product Assessment

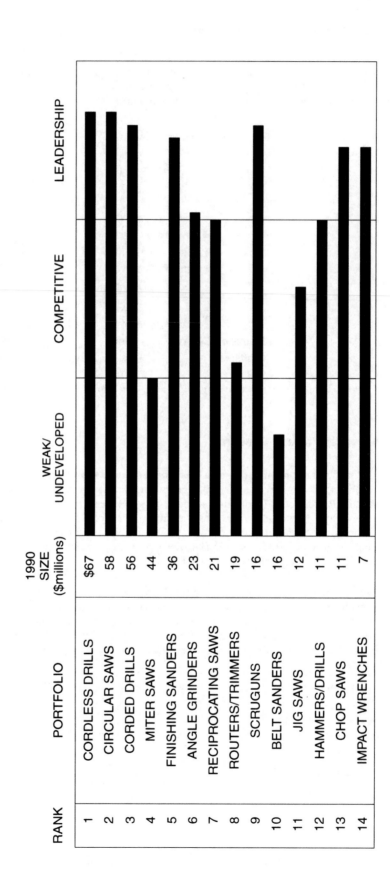

PROFESSIONAL POWER TOOL PRODUCT ASSESSMENT

RANK	PORTFOLIO	1990 SIZE ($millions)	WEAK/ UNDEVELOPED	COMPETITIVE	LEADERSHIP
1	CORDLESS DRILLS	$67			
2	CIRCULAR SAWS	58			
3	CORDED DRILLS	56			
4	MITER SAWS	44			
5	FINISHING SANDERS	36			
6	ANGLE GRINDERS	23			
7	RECIPROCATING SAWS	21			
8	ROUTERS/TRIMMERS	19			
9	SCRUGUNS	16			
10	BELT SANDERS	16			
11	JIG SAWS	12			
12	HAMMERS/DRILLS	11			
13	CHOP SAWS	11			
14	IMPACT WRENCHES	7			

Research on Brand Awareness and Perceptions

Telephone surveys and B&D's annual Image Study provided data on brand awareness, relative perceived quality, and ratings on specific attributes. Overall awareness of the major brands among the Professional-Tradesmen segment end users are shown in **Table B**.

Table B 1990 Total Awareness of Power Tool Suppliers
Among Tradespeople

Awareness			
Black & Decker	98%	Hitachi	77%
Milwaukee	95%	Hilti	73%
Skil	93%	Porter Cable	67%
Makita	90%	Ryobi	50%
Bosch	87%		

Respondents were also asked to state their level of agreement with the statement, "*Brand X is one of the Best.*" The data on percentage of respondents "agreeing" or "strongly agreeing" with the statement are in **Table C**.

Table C "One of the Best" Agreement Data

Milwaukee	80%
Makita	67%
Black & Decker	44%

The Image Study provided the same agree/strongly agree data at the level of specific attributes. In particular, **Table D** segregates those expressing a preference for Makita and those expressing a preference for Milwaukee and compares perceptions of those brands to perceptions of B&D.

Table D Percent Agreeing with the Statement

	Those Who Prefer Makita		Those Who Prefer Milwaukee	
	Makita	B&D	Milwaukee	B&D
Makes High-Quality Tools	82%	51%	91%	43%
Makes Durable/Rugged Tools	71%	48%	91%	42%
Proud to Own	78%	43%	86%	36%
Easy to Get Service	44%	67%	68%	66%
Stands Behind Products	56%	61%	69%	52%

As Galli reflected on the research data, he recalled some of the comments made to him by two tradesmen during site visits:

"... Black & Decker makes a good popcorn popper, and my wife just loves her Dustbuster, but I'm out here trying to make a living ..."

". . . On the job, people notice what you're working with . . . if I came out here with one of those Black & Decker gray things, I'd be laughed at."

Galli knew that a copycat strategy, e.g., paint it blue and spend some advertising dollars on a "Black & Decker as appropriate for the tradesmen" theme, would not receive internal support. Three options presented themselves:

Option 1. Harvest Professional-Tradesmen Channels

In this strategy, B&D would focus on the Consumer and the Professional-Industrial segments. In the Professional-Tradesmen segment, the focus would be on profitability even at the expense of market share.

Option 2. Get Behind Black & Decker Name with Sub-Branding

While there had been several half-hearted attempts to rebuild the B&D name in the Professional-Tradesmen segment, they had not been successful. One new aspect which might offer promise, though, was the sub-branding strategy, which had been so successful with the Spacemaker line and which Galli had used earlier in his career in the accessories business. Specifically, he had transitioned replacement saw blades from "Black & Decker" brand to "Piranha® by Black & Decker." (See **Exhibit 3**.) In 1990, B&D had introduced the Sawcat™ and Super Sawcat™ circular saws with some success. An intense sub-branding program could be developed in an integrated fashion.

Option 3. Drop the Black & Decker Name from the Professional-Tradesmen Segment

Galli imagined what internal reaction would be to such a proposal. Everyone had taken great pride in the #7 "brand power" position of the B&D name. As one of his colleagues commented to him, "Joe, it can't make sense to pull the name of the creator of the power tools industry from a power tool. You'd be saying that B&D can't make it in power tools. Besides, if General Electric can put its name on everything from jet engines to telephones, why can't we?"

If he were to propose dropping the B&D name, he would need an alternative. One possibility was to develop a new brand name free of any negative associations, similar to Toyota's creation of the Lexus brand. The other would be to use some other name already in B&D stable of brands. One of these possibilities was the DeWalt® brand from a line of stationary woodworking equipment. DeWalt was founded in 1918 and bought by Black & Decker in 1960. DeWalt was a leader in sales of large radial arm saws permanently installed at lumber yards. While sales of DeWalt products had reached $70 million annually at one time under B&D, the company had recently deemphasized the line due to the amount of product liability exposure that came with large, stationary woodworking equipment. The DeWalt name had never been used on a portable power tool.

The DeWalt name had been included in the awareness research described in **Table B** above. It received a 70% awareness rating, and most of those who knew DeWalt were positively disposed to it. Surprisingly, it had achieved an "Is One of the Best" agreement percent of 63% from tradesmen as compared to B&D's 44% (**Table C**). Further research on the DeWalt brand showed that 51% of tradespeople would have some "purchase interest." The "level of endorsement" by B&D impacted the "purchase interest" score. Specifically:

The Black & Decker Corporation (A): Power Tools Division 595-057

Identified As	% Purchase Interest
• DeWalt	51%
• DeWalt–Serviced and Distributed by Black & Decker	58%
• DeWalt–Manufactured, Serviced and Distributed by Black & Decker	53%

Galli felt that any plan involving investing to build market share—Option 2 or Option 3—would have to provide for a minimal objective of doubling B&D's Professional-Tradesmen segment share from under 10% to nearly 20% within three years, with major share "take-away" from Makita. Operating income would be expected to improve steadily from under 10% to at least 12%. He also knew that the Membership Clubs, which represented about 10% of segment sales for the industry were and would continue to be off-limits. Thus, he would not be able to attack the 85% share Makita held within that channel.

He wondered what type of reaction to expect from Makita if he pursued a "build share" option. Finally, he considered the risk. On the one hand, B&D was not making much money in the Professional-Tradesmen segment anyway, so financial risk was limited. On the other hand, there might be implications for the other two segments and embarrassment in the retail channels.

One of the color options he was considering was a bold "Industrial Yellow"—a familiar job site color associated with safety, but not yet used by any power tool brand. But, if the strategy was not success, Galli could not think of anything good that could come from his product being the same color as a lemon.

595-057   **The Black & Decker Corporation (A): Power Tools Division**

Exhibit 1 Market Shares of Professional-Tradesmen Tools by Product Type—1990

		Approximate Shares		
Product	**Approximate % of Market**	**Makita**	**Milwaukee**	**B&D**
• **Drills** (30%)				
- Cordless Drivers	16%	80%	<5%	<10%
- Corded	13%	50%	20%	25%
• **Saws** (35%)				
- Circular[a]	14%	55%	15%	<10%
- Miter	11%	45%	-	15%
- Reciprocating	<10%	30%	30%	25%
- Jig	<5%	25%	15%	<10%
- Chop	<5%	50%	<5%	20%
• **Sanders** (>15%)				
- Finishing	<10%	60%	<5%	<10%
- Belt[b]	<5%	20%	-	-

[a]Skil held approximately 20% of Circular Saws.
[b]Ryobi held approximately 45% of Belt Sanders.

Exhibit 2 Market Shares of Professional-Tradesmen by Channel Type—1990

		Approximate Shares Within Channel Type	
	Approximate % of Professional Segment Sales in This Channel	**Makita Share**	**B&D Share**
Two-Step	40%	55%	<10%
Home Centers	25%	45%	<10%
Warehouse Home Centers	15%	45%	20%
Membership Clubs	10%	85%	0%
Farm Outlets	5%	45%	15%

The Black & Decker Corporation (A): Power Tools Division   595-057

Exhibit 3   Piranha Sub-Brand

Harvard Business School

9-598-150

Rev. May 27, 1999

Biopure Corporation

It was February 5, 1998, as Carl Rausch, president and CEO of Biopure Corporation, opened his Boston Globe and read about the U.S. government's final approval of Oxyglobin (see **Exhibit 1**). Oxyglobin was the first of two new "blood substitutes" on which Biopure's future depended—Oxyglobin for the veterinary market and Hemopure for the human market. While Oxyglobin was ready for launch, Hemopure was still two years away from final government approval. This timing was the source of an ongoing debate within Biopure.

Ted Jacobs, vice president for Human Clinical Trials at Biopure, argued that the release of Oxyglobin should be delayed until *after* Hemopure was approved and had established itself in the marketplace (see **Exhibit 2** for an organizational chart of Biopure). Given that the two products were almost identical in physical properties and appearance, he felt that Oxyglobin would create an unrealistic price expectation for Hemopure if released first. As he made clear in a recent management meeting,

> ... [T]he veterinary market is small and price sensitive. We'll be lucky to get $150 per unit. The human market, on the other hand, is many times larger and we can realistically achieve price points of $600 to $800 per unit. But as soon as we come out with Oxyglobin at $150, we jeopardize our ability to price Hemopure at $800. Hospitals and insurance firms will be all over us to justify a 500% price difference for what they see as the same product. That's a headache we just don't need. We've spent $200 million developing Hemopure—to risk it at this point is crazy. We should just shelve Oxyglobin for now.

At the same time, Andy Wright, vice president for Veterinary Products, had his sales organization in place and was eager to begin selling Oxyglobin. He argued that the benefits of immediately releasing Oxyglobin outweighed the risks,

> Oxyglobin would generate our first revenues ever—revenues we could use to launch Hemopure. And while the animal market is smaller than the human market, it is still attractive. Finally, I can't stress enough the value of Oxyglobin in learning how to "go to market." Would you rather make the mistakes now, with Oxyglobin, or in two years, with Hemopure?

While Carl Rausch listened to this debate, he also considered his colleagues' growing desire to take Biopure public in the near future. He wondered whether a proven success with Oxyglobin might not have a greater impact on an IPO than the promise of success with Hemopure.

An Overview of Biopure

Biopure Corporation was founded in 1984 by entrepreneurs Carl Rausch and David Judelson as a privately owned biopharmaceutical firm specializing in the ultrapurification of proteins for human and veterinary use. By 1998, this mission had taken Biopure to the point where it was one of three legitimate contenders in the emerging field of "blood substitutes."[1] Blood substitutes were designed to replicate the oxygen-carrying function of actual blood, while eliminating the shortcomings associated with the transfusion of donated blood. Through the end of 1997, no blood substitute had received approval for use anywhere in the world.

Biopure's entries into this field were Hemopure, for the human market, and Oxyglobin, for the animal market. Both products consisted of the oxygen-carrying protein "hemoglobin" which had been removed from red blood cells, purified to eliminate infectious agents, and chemically modified to increase its safety and effectiveness. What distinguished Hemopure and Oxyglobin from other "hemoglobin-based" blood substitutes under development was the fact that they were "bovine-sourced" as opposed to "human-sourced"—they were derived from the blood of cattle. To date, Biopure had spent over $200 million in the development of Oxyglobin and Hemopure and in the construction of a state-of-the-art manufacturing facility.

Both of Biopure's products fell under the approval process of the United States government's Food and Drug Administration (FDA), which required that each product be proven safe and effective for medical use (see **Exhibit 3** for an overview of the FDA approval process). In this regard, Oxyglobin had just received final FDA approval for commercial release as a veterinary blood substitute, while Hemopure would soon enter Phase 3 clinical trials and was optimistically expected to see final FDA approval for release as a human blood substitute sometime in 1999.

This recent FDA approval of Oxyglobin brought to a peak a long-simmering debate within Biopure. With its primary goal being the development of a human blood substitute, Biopure's entry into the animal market had been somewhat opportunistic. During Pre-Clinical trials for Hemopure, the benefits of a blood substitute for small animals became apparent. In response, Biopure began a parallel product development process which resulted in Oxyglobin. However, there was little question within Biopure that Oxyglobin was an ancillary product to Hemopure.

As it became apparent that Oxyglobin would gain FDA approval prior to Hemopure, Carl Rausch and his management team discussed how best to manage Oxyglobin. As the first "blood substitute" of any type to receive full government approval, Rausch was eager to get the news out. With this in mind, Andy Wright and a small marketing team had been assembled to bring Oxyglobin to market. However, Ted Jacobs and others questioned whether the immediate release of Oxyglobin might not impinge on Biopure's ability to optimally price Hemopure. After months of debate, it was time to decide on the fate of Oxyglobin.

---

[1] While the term *blood substitute* has historically been used to describe this class of product, Biopure and the medical community increasingly have used the term *oxygen therapeutic* to describe the latest generation of product. For simplicity, however, we will continue to use the term *blood substitute* in this case.

Biopure Corporation   598-150

The Human Blood Market

Blood is essential for life. It performs many functions, the most acutely critical of which is the transportation of oxygen to the organs and tissues of the human body. Without oxygen, these organs and tissues will die within minutes.

That portion of blood responsible for oxygen transportation are the red blood cells (RBCs). RBCs capture inhaled oxygen from the lungs, carry that oxygen to the cells of the body, release it for use where needed, capture expended carbon dioxide from those cells, and carry that carbon dioxide back to the lungs, where it is released. The key to this process is "hemoglobin," the iron-containing protein found within each RBC to which oxygen and carbon dioxide molecules bind.

The adult human body contains 5,000 milliliters (ml) or about 10 pints of blood. An individual can naturally compensate for the loss of up to 30% of this volume through some combination of increased oxygen intake (i.e., faster breathing), increased flow of the remaining blood (i.e., faster heart rate) and the prioritization of blood delivery to vital organs. In cases of blood loss of greater than 30%, however, outside intervention is typically required—generally in the form of a "blood transfusion."

Human Blood Transfusions

A blood transfusion entails the direct injection of blood into a patient's bloodstream. As of 1998, the most common form of blood transfusion was the intravenous transfusion of donated RBCs.[2] Typically, a healthy individual would donate 1 unit or 500 ml of "whole" blood, which would be tested for various infectious diseases, sorted by blood type, and separated into its usable components (e.g., plasma, platelets, and RBCs). This process would yield 1 unit or 250 ml of RBCs, which then would be stored until needed by a patient. [3]

While potentially lifesaving, the transfusion of donated RBCs has limitations. These include

- The need for exact blood typing and cross-matching between donor and recipient. The RBCs of each human may contain specific blood sugars, or antigens. The existence or absence of these antigens creates a complex set of allowable transfusions between donor and recipient, as shown in **Exhibit 4**. Transfusions outside of those outlined can be fatal to the recipient.

- The reduced oxygen-carrying efficiency of stored RBCs. RBCs stored for 10 days or more are only about 50% efficient at transporting oxygen in the first 8 to 12 hours after transfusion.

- The limited shelf-life for stored RBCs. RBCs can be safely stored for only about 6 weeks, after which time they are typically discarded.

- The need for refrigeration. For optimal shelf-life, RBCs must be stored at 4° Celsius (~40° F).

---

[2] Historically, whole blood transfusions were the norm. Since the 1970s, however, whole blood increasingly had been separated into RBCs, platelets and plasma, allowing for (1) several patients to benefit from a single unit of donated blood and (2) a reduced likelihood of negative reaction for any given patient.

[3] In blood medicine, 1 unit is defined in terms of its therapeutic value. Therefore, "1 unit" or 250 ml of RBCs provides the oxygen-carrying capacity of "1 unit" or 500 ml of whole blood. Similarly, "1 unit" of a blood substitute (i.e., typically 125 ml) provides the same oxygen-carrying capacity of "1 unit" of RBCs or whole blood.

- The risk of disease transmission. While donated blood is tested for infectious agents, there still exists the risk of disease transmission. For example, the risk of AIDS is 1:500,000, the risk of Hepatitis B is 1:200,000, and the risk of Hepatitis C is 1:100,000.

Autologous transfusions   In an attempt to overcome some of these limitations, the use of "autologous" or self-donated RBCs has become increasingly common. In an autologous RBC transfusion, a medically stable patient who anticipates the need for RBCs would have his or her own blood drawn weeks in advance, separated into its components, and saved until needed. Research has shown this process to significantly reduce a patient's rate of complication and post-operative infection, thereby hastening recovery and shortening his or her stay in the hospital.

Human Blood Supply and Demand

Human blood supply   Fourteen million units of RBCs were donated by 8 million people in 1995 in the United States. Approximately 12.9 million of these units came from individuals who voluntarily donated to one of over 1,000 nonprofit blood collection organizations. By far, the largest of these organizations was the American Red Cross, which collected half of all the blood donated in the United States in 1995 through a network of 44 regional blood collection centers. Typically, the Red Cross and the other blood collection organizations supported "blood mobiles," which traveled to high schools, colleges, and places of employment to reach potential donors. The remaining 1.1 million units of RBCs were autologous donations made directly to a hospital blood center.

Increasingly, blood collection was a struggle. While 75% of all adults qualified as a donor, fewer than 5% actually donated in a given year. Historically, reasons for donating included altruism and peer pressure, while reasons for not donating included fear of needles and lack of time. Since the mid-1980s, an additional reason for not donating involved the misconception that donating put one at risk for contracting AIDS. Public education had failed to counteract this misconception.

Given the low rate of donation and the relatively short shelf-life of RBCs, it was not uncommon for medical facilities and blood banks to experience periodic shortages of RBCs. This was especially true during the winter holidays and the summer months, periods which routinely displayed both increased demand and decreased rates of donation.

Human blood demand   Of the 14 million units of RBCs donated in 1995, 2.7 million were discarded due to contamination or expiration (i.e., units older than 6 weeks). Another 3.2 million units were transfused into 1.5 million patients who suffered from chronic anemia, an ongoing deficiency in the oxygen-carrying ability of the blood. The remaining 8.1 million units were transfused into 2.5 million patients who suffered from acute blood loss brought on by elective surgeries, emergency surgeries, or trauma. Exhibit 5 offers a breakdown of RBC transfusions in 1995.

In elective and emergency surgeries, RBCs were routinely transfused in situations where blood loss was greater than two units, as was typical in heart bypass and organ transplant surgeries. In surgeries with blood loss of one to two units, however, RBCs typically were not transfused in spite of their potential benefit. In these "borderline" transfusion surgeries, doctors typically avoided transfusions for fear of disease transmission or negative reaction caused by the transfused RBCs. There were approximately 1 million "borderline transfusion" surgeries in the United States each year.

RBC transfusions were also required in the approximate 500,000 trauma cases which occurred every year in the United States. These cases were characterized by the massive loss of blood due to automobile accidents, gunshot wounds, etc. However, due to the resources required to store, type, and administer RBCs, only 10% of trauma victims received RBCs "in the field" or at the site of the accident. Blood transfusions for the remaining 90% of victims were delayed until the victim arrived at a hospital emergency room. This delay was often cited as a contributing factor to the 30% fatality rate seen in these trauma cases, as evidenced by the 20,000 trauma victims who bled to death each year prior to reaching the hospital. As one doctor put it,

> ... [T]hose first few minutes after a trauma are known as the "Golden Hour."
> Life and death often depends on how fast the lost blood is replaced in this period.

Looking forward, while the demand for RBCs to treat chronic anemia was expected to remain stable, the demand for RBCs to treat acute blood loss was expected to rise with the aging U.S. population. Individuals over 65 years of age comprised 15% of the adult population in 1995 and received over 40% of all "acute blood loss" transfusions. By the year 2030, this over-65 segment was expected to double in absolute numbers and to grow to 25% of the adult population.

Human blood pricing   Since the AIDS crisis, it has been illegal for an individual to sell his or her blood in the United States. As such, all blood donations are unpaid. In turn, to cover their expense of collection and administration, blood collection organizations sell this donated blood to hospitals and medical centers. Once obtained, hospitals incur additional costs to store, handle, transport, screen, type, cross-match and document the blood. Estimates for these costs are outlined in Exhibit 6. Typically, these costs are passed on to the patient or to the patient's insurance provider.

The Veterinary Blood Market

The role of RBCs for animals is biologically identical to its role for humans: RBCs transport oxygen to an animal's tissues and organs. In practice, however, the availability and transfusion of blood was considerably more constrained in the veterinary market than it was in the human market.

Veterinary market structure   There were approximately 15,000 small-animal veterinary practices in the United States in 1995. Of these, about 95% were "primary care" practices which provided preventative care (e.g., shots, checkups), routine treatment of illness (e.g., infections, chronic anemia), and limited emergency care (e.g., simple surgery and trauma). The remaining 5% of practices were "emergency care" or "specialty care" practices. Approximately 75% of primary care practices referred some or all of their major surgery and severe trauma cases to these emergency care practices. Across both the primary care and emergency care practices, patient volume was concentrated in dogs (~50% of patient volume) and cats (~35% of volume). Exhibit 7 provides a staffing and patient profile of small-animal veterinary clinics in the United States.

Veterinary blood demand   In practice, blood transfusions in the veterinary market were infrequent. In 1995, for example, the average veterinary practice was presented with 800 dogs suffering from acute blood loss. About 30% of these dogs would have benefited significantly from a transfusion of blood, but only about 2.5% were deemed "critical cases" and received a transfusion.

The incidence of these acute blood loss cases was relatively concentrated, with 15% of veterinary practices handling 65% of all canine surgeries and 10% of practices handling 55% of all canine trauma cases. Not surprisingly, these "high incident" practices tended to be the larger primary care practices and the emergency care practices. This concentration was also evident in blood transfusions. In 1995, an average of 17 units of canine blood were transfused by each primary care practice, while an average of 150 units were transfused by each emergency care practice.

Veterinary blood supply[4]   Historically, the biggest constraint to veterinary transfusions was the lack of an adequate blood supply. In contrast to the human market, there existed few animal blood

---

[4] Unlike the human market, transfusions in the animal market still tended to be "whole blood" transfusions.

banks. As a result, the sole source of blood for most veterinary practices were donor animals which were housed at the practice for the expressed purpose of donating blood. When a dog or cat was in need of blood, blood was drawn from a donor dog or cat and then transfused into the animal in need. For primary care practices, donor animals provided 93% of all transfused blood, while blood banks provided the remaining 7%. In emergency practices, these proportions were 78% and 22%.

About 15% of veterinary practices found the "donor animal" system to be administratively or financially prohibitive and did not offer it as a service. Of the 85% of practices that did use a donor system, few had a good sense of its cost. In particular, few practices explicitly tracked the cost of housing the donor animal or the time required to draw the blood. As a proxy for these costs, practices typically looked to the price of a unit of blood from an animal blood bank. In 1995, that cost was $50 to $100. In turn, a typical primary care practice charged a pet owner $80 to $120 per unit and a typical emergency care practice charged a pet owner $130 to $170 per unit.

Finally, most practices that conducted transfusions lacked the time and resources to properly type both the donor and recipient blood. According to one estimate, only one-tenth of practices reported always typing the blood of both the donor and recipient animal. While complications due to incompatible blood types were not nearly as severe for dogs as they are for humans, this lack of blood typing and cross-matching was shown to prolong the recovery of a patient animal.

These factors resulted in many veterinarians viewing the transfusion of animal blood as the treatment of last resort, with 84% of veterinary doctors reporting overall dissatisfaction with the blood transfusion alternatives currently available in the marketplace.

Human Blood Substitutes

Originally conceived as a vehicle to treat wounded soldiers in battlefield settings, the potential for a human blood substitute for nonmilitary use became increasingly apparent since the 1950s. This period saw a significant rise in auto accidents, the advent of open heart and organ transplant surgeries, and the AIDS crisis, which called into question the safety of the blood supply.

By 1998, several companies appeared to be on the verge of a viable blood substitute with a class of product called "hemoglobin-based blood substitutes." These products attempted to exploit the natural oxygen-carrying capabilities of hemoglobin while eliminating the limitations associated with donated RBCs. Each of these companies was attempting to (1) extract the hemoglobin found within human or animal RBCs, (2) purify that hemoglobin to eliminate infectious agents, and (3) modify the otherwise unstable free hemoglobin molecule to prevent it from breaking down. These purification and modification processes were nontrivial and represented the bulk of blood substitute research conducted over the past 20 years.

Product benefits   In theory, these hemoglobin-based blood substitutes eliminated many of the limitations associated with donated RBCs. In particular, they were

- "Universal" blood substitutes, eliminating the need for blood typing and cross-matching.

- Free of infectious agents and contamination.

- Increased shelf life. These blood substitutes could be safely stored for up to 2 years.

- Immediately 100% efficient at transporting oxygen. Unlike whole RBCs, modified hemoglobin did not require a period of time to achieve peak oxygen-carrying efficiency.

In addition to these "anticipated" benefits, hemoglobin-based blood substitutes were displaying several "unanticipated" benefits which companies were only just beginning to investigate. In particular, given that hemoglobin molecules were significantly smaller than RBCs, they were able to flow to regions of the body that RBCs might not be able to reach. It was believed that this could lead to improved treatments in cases of stroke and heart attack—cases where RBCs often were slowed or restricted from reaching vital organs either due to artery blockages or decreased blood pressure.

Product shortcomings   At the same time, these "hemoglobin-based" blood substitutes did have some shortcomings, including:

- A short half-life.   While donated RBCs remained in the body for up to two months after transfusion, these blood substitutes were excreted from the body within 2 to 7 days.

- The potential for higher toxicity.   While the human body could tolerate the limitless and continuous replacement of one's blood with donated blood, the safety of these blood substitutes had been demonstrated only up to transfusion levels of 5 to 10 units.

In spite of these shortcomings, Dr. C. Everett Koop, the former Surgeon General of the United States, proclaimed,

> When the history of 20th-century medicine is written, the development of blood substitutes will be listed among the top ten advances in medicine. ... [B]ecause of its purity, efficacy and convenience, this product class has the potential to revolutionize the practice of medicine, especially in critical-care situations. ... [T]he next generation will not know how tough it was for those of us in medical practice before this technology became available. [5]

Others were less optimistic. One industry analyst presented a less attractive scenario for hemoglobin-based blood substitutes:

> ... [W]e feel that there is no urgent need for blood substitutes since donated human blood is, for the most part, safe and effective. The expectation that blood substitutes will command vast markets and high price premiums is based on the assumptions that blood substitutes will prove safer and more effective than donated blood. While only time will tell if this is true, it will be an uphill battle given the widespread acceptance of donated blood.

The FDA Approval Process

Human blood substitutes fell under the strict regulation of the U.S. government's Food and Drug Administration (FDA), which required that a product be proven safe and effective for medical use before being approved for commercial release (refer back to **Exhibit 3**). By early 1998, three companies had products that were in the final stages of this process. These products differed in their source of raw hemoglobin and in the process by which that hemoglobin was purified and modified. The FDA approval process was sensitive to these differences. Short of beginning the FDA approval process anew, each company was limited in its ability to substantially alter either the source of their hemoglobin or the process by which that hemoglobin was purified and modified. In addition, given that most of the companies had patented their purification and modification processes, there was little opportunity for a new entrant to quickly gain FDA approval.

---

[5] Biopure company website.

Competitors for a Human Blood Substitute

As of 1998, Baxter International and Northfield Laboratories were the only other companies in late-stage development of a hemoglobin-based blood substitute. All other competitors were either several years behind in their development of a hemoglobin-based product or were pursuing a less promising technology.

In contrast to Biopure's use of cattle as its source of hemoglobin, both Baxter and Northfield relied on human blood as their source of hemoglobin. In particular, both companies had developed a technology to extract raw hemoglobin from "outdated" human RBCs (i.e., RBCs intended for transfusion, but which had been stored for more than 6 weeks). While their production processes and their pending FDA approval did not preclude them from using fresh RBCs, it was the stated intention of both companies to initially rely on outdated human RBCs. Through 1998, Baxter had an agreement with the American Red Cross to obtain outdated RBCs at a cost of $8 per unit. Until recently, Northfield had a similar $8 per unit agreement with Blood Centers of America, another national blood collection agency. However, in early 1997, Blood Centers of America raised their price to Northfield to $26 per unit for outdated RBCs.

In addition to their reliance on human blood, the products of Baxter and Northfield also differed from Biopure's in that they needed to be frozen or refrigerated until used. Biopure's Hemopure was shelf-stable at room temperature.

Baxter International   With over $5.4 billion in sales and $670 million in net income in 1996, Baxter was an acknowledged leader in the development, manufacture and sale of blood-related medical products, ranging from artificial heart valves to blood-collection equipment. In addition, Baxter had a long history of product breakthrough, having developed the first sterile blood collection device in 1939, the first commercially available artificial kidney machine in 1956, and the first Factor VIII blood-clotting factor for the treatment of hemophilia in 1966.

"HemAssist," Baxter's patented blood substitute, was expected to add to this string of breakthroughs. Representing 30 years and $250 million in effort, HemAssist was the first human blood substitute to proceed to Phase 3 clinical trials in June 1996. Initially, these trials were expected to lead to full FDA approval by late 1998. However, in October 1997, Baxter revised its estimate to late 1999 or early 2000—an announcement that was followed by a 10% dip in Baxter's stock price.

Despite this delay, Baxter recently constructed a $100 million facility with a production capacity of 1 million units of HemAssist per year. Aside from its variable cost of source material, Baxter was expected to incur production costs of approximately $50 million per year, independent of production volume. While still just industry speculation, it was anticipated that Baxter would price HemAssist between $600 and $800 per unit.

Northfield Laboratories   Northfield Laboratories of Illinois also had recently entered Phase 3 trials with a hemoglobin-based blood substitute. Northfield's product, "PolyHeme," was very similar to Baxter's HemAssist in its production and usage profile. Based on early positive results from its Phase 3 trials, Northfield anticipated full FDA approval in late 1999.

In contrast to Baxter, Northfield was a small, 45-person firm that was founded in 1985 for the sole purpose of developing a human blood substitute. As such, PolyHeme represented its only product. Analysts expected PolyHeme to be priced comparably to HemAssist upon release.

By early 1998, Northfield had spent $70 million in its development of PolyHeme and in the construction of a pilot production facility with an output capacity of 10,000 units per year. While this facility was sufficient to satisfy demand during clinical trials, Northfield management recognized the need for a full-scale production facility. With this in mind, they hoped to construct a $45 million facility with a capacity of 300,000 units per year. With this factory in place, aside from the cost of raw material, production costs were expected to be about $30 million per year, independent of production volume. By early 1998, selection of a factory site and plant construction had not yet begun.

Animal Blood Substitutes

Through early 1998, Biopure was the only company that was actively engaged in the development of a blood substitute for the small-animal veterinary market. And while there was little to prevent Baxter or Northfield (or anyone else) from attempting to enter the veterinary market, any company wishing to do so would have to initiate an FDA-approval process specific to the veterinary market. By one estimate, assuming a company immediately began such a process, it would take 2 to 5 years to bring a product to market.

Biopure and Its Blood Substitutes

Hemopure and Oxyglobin were nearly identical in terms of physical characteristics and production processes. The only difference between the two products was in the size of the hemoglobin "clusters" that were contained in the final products. In the production of Oxyglobin, both large and small clusters of hemoglobin molecules were naturally formed. However, the small clusters tended to cause minor gastrointestinal problems and discoloration of urine. While considered acceptable in the animal market, these side effects were undesirable in the human market. As a result, Hemopure followed the same production process as used to make Oxyglobin, with a final step added to remove the small hemoglobin clusters.

Biopure had a single manufacturing facility, with an output capacity varying by the production mix of Oxyglobin and Hemopure. The same equipment was used to produce either product, but only one product could be produced at a time. This resulted in an annual capacity of 300,000 units of Oxyglobin or 150,000 units of Hemopure or some linear combination inbetween. The lower output for Hemopure reflected the facts that (1) the added step to remove the small hemoglobin clusters decreased the rate of production, and (2) the removal of the small hemoglobin clusters decreased yield.

To support these levels of output, aside from the cost of raw material, Biopure anticipated overall production costs of $15 million per year, independent of volume. For raw material, it anticipated a ready supply of bovine blood priced at $1.50 per unit. Biopure paid this money to cattle slaughterhouses to collect and transport the blood of cattle that were being processed for their meat—blood that otherwise would have been discarded. It was estimated that 10,000 cattle could supply enough raw material to support full production in Biopure's existing manufacturing facility.

Status of Hemopure

As of early 1998, Hemopure was in Phase 3 clinical trials in Europe, with FDA approval for Phase 3 trials in the United States appearing imminent. In anticipation of this approval, Biopure had established sites for Phase 3 trials and was ready to proceed immediately upon approval. While acknowledging the potential pitfalls of any clinical trials, Biopure was confident that the Phase 3 trials would be successful and that the FDA would grant full approval sometime in 1999. Biopure expected to commercially release Hemopure sometime in late 1999 or early 2000.

In line with the anticipated price of Baxter's HemAssist, Biopure planned to price Hemopure at $600 to $800 per unit. However, little systematic testing had been done by Biopure to determine the acceptability of these prices. In particular, little was known of the price sensitivity of medical personnel, insurance providers, or of patients when it came to human blood substitutes.

Status of Oxyglobin

In 1997, Biopure established the Veterinary Products Division and hired Andy Wright to oversee the marketing and sale of Oxyglobin. Working under the assumption that Biopure would begin selling Oxyglobin immediately upon approval, Wright faced a host of decisions, including how to price and how to distribute Oxyglobin. Supporting him in these decisions was a team of seven employees—one director of marketing, one technical service representative (to answer technical questions and complaints), two customer service representatives (to support ordering and billing), and three sales representatives (to make sales calls and generate orders).

The pricing of Oxyglobin   Some members of Wright's sales team argued for Oxyglobin to be priced at $80 to $100 per unit. These team members pointed to the price sensitivity of the vet market, arguing that few pet owners carried health insurance on their animals. They also noted that the average cost of a visit to the vet was only about $60, with few procedures costing more than $100 (see Exhibit 8). Finally, they noted that vets tended to use a simple "doubling rule" when pricing a medical product to the pet owners, bringing the end-user price of Oxyglobin to $160 to $200 per unit.

Other members of Andy Wright's sales team felt that Oxyglobin should carry a premium price of up to $200 per unit, reflecting the many advantages of Oxyglobin relative to donated animal blood. These team members pointed out that while the average cost of a visit to a primary care practice might be only $60, the cost of a visit to an emergency care practice could easily run from $200 to over $1,000. They also questioned whether veterinary doctors would just blindly double the price of Oxyglobin without regard for its high dollar contribution. Finally, they noted that at a low price, Biopure could never hope to recoup the massive cost of product development.

To better understand the channel's willingness to pay for an animal blood substitute, Biopure conducted two surveys in 1997—one survey of 285 veterinarians and another of 200 dog owners. **Table A** offers results of the veterinarian survey and **Table B** offers results of the owner survey.

In reviewing these surveys, Wright reminded himself that veterinarians often played the role of gatekeeper when it came to potential treatments, recommending less-expensive over more-expensive treatments in an effort to save their clients' money. At the same time, 90% of pet owners reported that they wanted to be made fully aware of all the alternatives available to treat their pets.

Table A   Veterinarians' Reported Willingness to Trial Oxyglobin

Price to Veterinarian	% of Veterinarians Who Would Trial Product	
	Noncritical Cases	**Critical Cases**
$50 per unit	95%	100%
$100 per unit	70%	95%
$150 per unit	25%	80%
$200 per unit	5%	60%

Source: Biopure company records

Table B Pet Owners' Willingness to Trial Oxyglobin

Price to Pet Owner	% of Pet Owners Who Would Trial Product	
	Noncritical Cases	**Critical Cases**
$100 per unit	60%	90%
$200 per unit	40%	85%
$300 per unit	35%	75%
$400 per unit	30%	65%

Source: Biopure company records

The distribution of Oxyglobin   Andy Wright also had to decide how best to sell and distribute Oxyglobin and how to educate veterinarians on its use.   In approaching this question, he looked to the current distribution practices for medical products in the veterinary market.

In 1997, $1.2 billion worth of product was sold to veterinary practices through a network of 200 independent distributors—each of whom sold and distributed the products of many manufacturers. Two of these independent distributors were national in scope, 18 were regional (e.g., New England), and 180 were local (e.g., metropolitan Boston). **Table C** provides a sales and staffing profile for these distributors. A manufacturer might contract with one national distributor, several nonoverlapping regional distributors, and many nonoverlapping local distributors. In return for their selling and distribution efforts, a distributor would receive 20% of the manufacturer selling price on a more-established product and 30% of the selling price on a less-established or new product.

Table C Profile of Independent Distributors of Veterinary Medicines

Type of Distributor	Number	% of Total Sales	Avg. Number of Sales Reps
National	2	25%	100
Regional	18	60%	40
Local	180	15%	1.5

Source: Biopure company records

A veterinary practice could expect one 15-minute visit per week from the sales representatives of its primary distributor. These 15-minute visits would entail a focused discussion of current promotions on existing products and a more limited discussion of products new to the market. Typically, a sales rep might introduce 100 new products in a given year. To educate a particular distributor's sales reps on a new product, a manufacturer might set up a series of training sessions. These training sessions would be conducted for groups of about 10 sales representatives each and last anywhere from 1 to 4 hours, depending on the complexity of the new product.

Another $300 million worth of products were sold directly to veterinary practices through manufacturer salesforces. Termed "manufacturer direct," this type of distribution often was used by manufacturers with either high-volume, well-established products or products which required a very sophisticated sales pitch. If Biopure chose this route, in addition to the cost of maintaining a salesforce, Andy estimated the cost to physically distribute Oxyglobin to be $10 to $15 per unit.

Andy Wright also considered trade publications and trade shows as another means by which to educate veterinarians about the existence and benefits of Oxyglobin. A quick investigation revealed that five journals had almost universal coverage across veterinarians and tended to be well-read. In addition, six large veterinary trade shows held in the United States each year attracted 2,000 to 10,000 veterinarians each. Typically, these trade shows were taken seriously by attendees and were a valued source of information. Andy wondered if either of these avenues made sense for Biopure.

Biopure's Decisions

While Andy dealt with the question of how best to market Oxyglobin, Carl Rausch wrestled with the larger question of whether and when to launch Oxyglobin. Should he listen to Ted Jacobs and postpone the launch of Oxyglobin until *after* Hemopure had established itself in the marketplace? Or should he listen to Andy and immediately launch Oxyglobin and reap the near-term benefits?

Not lost on Carl was the potential impact of Oxyglobin on a possible initial public offering of Biopure stock. To this point, Biopure had remained a privately held firm with very little debt. And while they currently had no revenues, a recent round of capital venture financing had provided them with $50 million—enough money to support operations for another two years. Nevertheless, many stakeholders in Biopure were anxious to take the company public. In this regard, Carl wondered whether a veterinary product with small but steady sales might not prove more attractive to investors than a human product still under development. He was especially sensitive to this issue in light of some recent, high-profile product failures in the Massachusetts biotechnology community (see **Exhibit 9**).

With all of this in mind, as president and CEO of Biopure, Carl Rausch pondered how best to leverage the opportunity offered by Oxyglobin without jeopardizing the potential of Hemopure.

Exhibit 1   Excerpts from *The Boston Globe* Article, February 5, 1998

Biopure's Blood Substitute for Dogs OK'd

Veterinarians scrambling to find blood for badly injured dogs now have a blood substitute. Biopure Corp. of Cambridge said yesterday it received federal regulatory approval to market oxygen-carrying blood derived from the blood of cows.

Tested in over 250 dogs, the company's blood substitute, called Oxyglobin, is initially aimed at the [canine blood transfusion market], according to Andrew W. Wright, vice president of Biopure's veterinary products.

The US Food and Drug Administration approval makes Oxyglobin the first blood substitutes for dogs, designed for dogs needing blood transfusions because of blood loss from accidents, surgeries, parasite infections, or rare anemia cases.

"This is breakthrough development because it quickly gets oxygen into tissue and organs and buys time for the dog's own regenerative red blood cells to come back," said Dr. Robert Murtaugh, professor of veterinary medicine and section head for emergency and critical care services at the Tufts University School of Veterinary Medicine.

The canine version is designed to largely replace drawing blood from donor dogs some veterinarians use in emergency situations.

Unlike blood that contains red blood cells, Biopure's technology uses a highly purified bovine hemoglobin that does not require blood typing or cross-matching. [Oxyglobin] can be stored in a veterinarian's storage area at room temperature for up to two years. A single bag—equivalent to a pint of whole blood—is sufficient for small to medium-sized dogs; two bags might be needed for larger dogs.

Reprinted with courtesy of *The Boston Globe.*

Exhibit 2   The Organizational Structure at Biopure Corporation

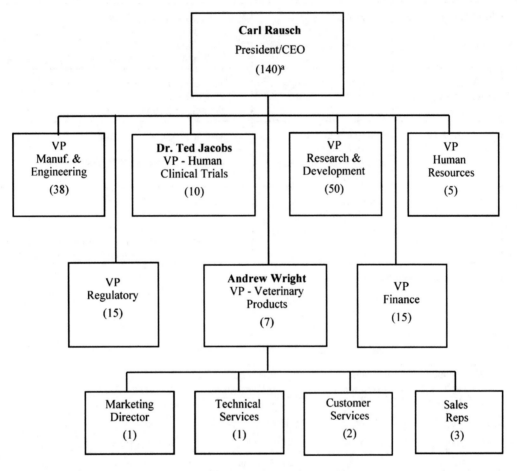

Source: Biopure company records

[a] Numbers in parenthesis represents the total number of employees that fall under a particular position's span of control. Thus, 140 employees either directly or indirectly report to Carl Rausch.

Exhibit 3   The United States FDA Approval Process

Phase	Goals	Characteristics
Pre-Clinical Trials	Safety in animals	– Typical length = 5 - 10 years – Need to show safety – Hope to show efficacy – Testing animals include mice, rats, dogs, sheep, etc.
Phase 1 Clinical Trials	Safety in healthy human subjects	– Typical length = 2 - 3 years – 20 - 100 individuals – Single-site testing location
Phase 2A & 2B Clinical Trials	2A - Safety in human patients 2B - Safety & efficacy in human patients	– Typical length = 1 - 2 years – 100 - 200 individuals – Single-site or multi-site testing locations
Phase 3 Clinical Trials	Large-scale safety & efficacy In use	– Typical length = 1 - 2 years – 100 - 500 individuals – Multi-site testing locations – Double-blind testing (i.e., neither patient nor doctor aware of specific product or brand)

Source: Biopure company records

Exhibit 4   Human Blood Typing and Allowable Transfusions[a]

Donor Blood Type	% of Population	Acceptable Recipients
AB	4%	AB[b]
A	40%	A, AB
B	11%	B, AB
O[c]	45%	O, A, B, AB

Source: The American Red Cross

[a] In addition to ABO blood typing, RBCs are either Rh+ or Rh-, further complicating allowable transfusions.

[b] AB is often referred to as the "universal recipient."

[c] O is often referred to as the "universal donor."

Biopure Corporation

Exhibit 5 Red Blood Cell Donations and Transfusions in
the United States in 1995

Use of Red Blood Cells	Units (in 000s)
Acute Blood Loss:	
Elective Surgery:	
Anonymous Donations	5,800
Autologous Donations [a,b]	1,100
Emergency Surgery (in hospital)	1,000
Trauma (in field administration)	200
Acute Blood Loss Subtotal	**8,100**
Chronic Anemia	**3,200**
Not Transfused	
Due to Rejection	1,200
Due to Expiration	1,500
Not Transfused Subtotal	**2,700**
Total:	**14,000**

Source: Stover & Associates LLC

[a] Autologous donations are in elective surgery only. All other uses
of RBCs represent anonymous donations.

[b] Autologous donations include both those units transfused and
those unused units discarded.

Exhibit 6 Cost to Patient of Donated Human Blood

	Low Estimate (per Unit)	High Estimate (per Unit)
Anonymous Donations:		
Hospital Acquisition Cost	$ 75	$150
Screening/Typing/Crossmatching	25	40
Transportation/Administration	25	35
Final Price of Anonymous	**$125**	**$225**
Autologous Donations:		
Added Administration and Handling	+ 150	+ 200
Final Price of Autologous	**$275**	**$425**

Source: Stover & Associates, LLC

Biopure Corporation   598-150

Exhibit 7 Profile of the 15,000 Veterinary Practices in the United States (1995)

Class of Practice	Average No. of Doctors	Relative Frequency	Average Monthly Case Load			Average Gross Revenues
			Dogs	Cats	Other	
Primary Care:						
1 Doctor Practices	1	25%	200	125	80	$265,000
2 Doctor Practices	2	30%	300	200	120	$460,000
3+ Doctor Practices	4.6	40%	450	300	160	$800,000
Average Primary Care	**2.7**	**95%**	**412**	**265**	**140**	**$570,000**
Emergency Care:						
Avg. Emergency Care	**4.0**	**5%**	**400**	**240**	**130**	**$770,000**

Source: Biopure Company Records

Exhibit 8 Small-Animal Veterinary Fees for Typical Procedures in Primary Care Practices in 1995

Procedure	Average Fee
Average Charge per Visit	***$58***
Office Call—Average Minimum Charge	$25
Boarding	$10
Hospitalization	$19
Anesthesia	$45
X-rays	$40
Blood Transfusion	$100
Hysterectomy	$80
Heartworm treatment	$250
Annual Vaccinations	$27
Rabies Vaccination	$12
Lab Tests—Average	$23
Dental Cleaning	$75
Deworming	$15

Source: *Veterinary Economics*, October, 1996, p. 45

Exhibit 9   Massachusetts Biopharmaceutical Companies' Proposed Drugs Sidelined in the 2nd Quarter, 1997

Firm/location	Date	Problem	Status of company
ImmunoGen Norwood, MA	March 18	Oncolysin B cancer drug halted after Phase 3 trial failure	Significantly downsized operations, extensive layoffs, major restructuring, sold biomanufacturing plant, and relocated corporate offices
OraVax Cambridge, MA	March 19	HNK20, a nosedrop designed to reduce hospitalization for lower respiratory infections caused by respiratory virus in infants, failed in a pivotal overseas clinical trial	Layoff of 20 people in April as part of a corporate reorganization
AutoImmune Lexington, MA	April 21	Myloral, an oral multiple sclerosis drug, did no better than placebo in Phase 3 trial	Major restructuring, now employs 20, down from 90 employees
Genzyme Cambridge, MA	May 5	Sepracoat, a surgical antiadhesion coating, was rejected by FDA advisory committee for lack of sufficient evidence of clinical effectiveness	Company selling Sepracoat in Europe; has FDA approval on related Seprafilm product
Cambridge Neuroscience Cambridge, MA	June 24	Cerestat clinical trial is halted over safety concerns by corporate partner, Boehringer Ingelheim	Six-month investigation begins to find reasons for concern

Source: *The Boston Globe*

SABRE Simulation

Student Guide

Version 3.2

Developed by

IIBD Ltd.

www.iibd.com   *+1 250-595-8440*   *info@iibd.com*

SABRE Market Simulation - Student's Guide

Version 3.2

This student guide is intended to provide a general overview of how to use SABRE and how the simulations work. You will also receive information specific to your simulation, either in the form of another document or in-class presentation, which details the marketplace in which you will be running your simulated company.

1.0   Introduction

SABRE is a flexible business simulation program that allows course instructors to design and run highly customized simulations. Its name stands for "**S**trategic **A**llocation of **B**usiness **RE**sources". SABRE allows up to six teams to compete against each other, as companies, for profits and market share. Each team operates its company by making decisions regarding product development, production, advertising and sales.

The simulation typically is run over six to ten periods, which you will treat as years or quarters. With that relatively long simulated timeframe and many decisions to be made, you and your team will have the opportunity to develop and implement your marketing strategies, and see the results. SABRE emphasizes the main elements of marketing strategy, and provides the framework for the overall decision-making and business planning process.

To be successful, you will have to work effectively as a team, as you must in real life. Each team starts with different strengths and weaknesses, as is also true in real life. It will be important to recognize your company's strengths and use them to your competitive advantage.

As you read through this introduction, you are beginning to participate in an exciting learning experience. You'll feel the frustration associated with failure and the rush of excitement when your team is successful. You will be challenged and, to be successful, you must constantly look for new opportunities to serve your market and gain competitive advantage. There will be emotional ups and downs but, as in any memorable experience, these are a necessity.

Section 2 describes the essential terms and concepts used in the simulation. Then the steps to getting SABRE up and running are presented in Section 3. Section 4 covers how to access information in SABRE and Section 5 describes the process to make decisions for your company.

2.0   Key Concepts and Terms

The business context of your simulation will be described by your instructor, or simulation "administrator". This section describes, in general, how a simulation works and some of the key terms. The specific market dynamics and sensitivities to various parameters will depend on the particular simulation.

In the simulation, you will be operating a company within a structure that views the scope of your responsibility as a profit center. Your company is rewarded each year with a budget that is a percentage of your net profits, subject to a minimum and a maximum. These floor and ceiling values and the percentage that you receive are specific to your simulation. You are not allowed to go over budget, so you must make tough resource allocation decisions. Where and how the budget is allocated is the execution of your strategy.

2.1 *Financial Performance*

Sales, less cost of goods sold, less all marketing and other expenses, gives the company's profit for the period. Your firm will receive the following information each period:

```
        Total Sales Revenue
  less  Cost of Goods Sold
    =   Gross Profit
------------------------------------------------
Basic Expenses
   advertising
   market research studies
   research and development
   sales force
plus Other Expenses
   inventory holding costs
   excess inventory sales cost
   =    Total Expenses
------------------------------------------------
NET PROFIT =  Gross Profit - Total Expenses
```

In the calculation of net profit above, the "Basic Expenses" must be covered within your budget for the period. However, the "Other Expenses" are not budget-affecting – they are applied outside the constraints of your company's budget.

2.2 *Markets and Segments*

You will be competing with other teams in either one or two *Markets*. Markets differ in the general type of *Product* being sold. The consumers in each market are grouped into *Segments*. Segments will be defined and shown as groups of customers with similar needs and wants. Each market has a set of *Attributes* (e.g. price, weight, speed, etc.) that describe the products in that market. Each segment has a different preference as to the ideal product. Those ideal attributes for each segment specify the segment's *Ideal Point*. These ideal points will move over time as the market evolves, and the segment sizes will also change. *It is crucial to understand that an individual will be more inclined to buy a product that best matches their ideal point.*

2.3 *Reports and Studies*

Every company receives a set of *Reports* (they're free!) each period which describe the company's performance and summarizes its situation. Additionally, companies receive the *Studies* that they purchased in the previous period, using money from their budget. Each study is specific to a market, and conveys information needed to make decisions. Section 5.4 describes the studies in detail, and examples of the Reports and Studies are provided in Appendix A.

2.4 Products and R&D Projects

As a company, you will put products on the market for sale. Every product is based on an *R&D Project*. That R&D project defines the underlying physical attributes of the product (e.g. weight, speed, etc.). More than one product can be based on a single R&D project.

The cost of an R&D project will depend on the unit cost of production you wish to attain for the product, and the attribute values. The lower the target unit cost, the higher the cost of the R&D project.

Before a product can be launched based on an R&D project, the R&D project must be funded and completed. The R&D project can be completed over one or several periods, and includes the up-front costs to prepare to offer a product or service to the market. (e.g. physical design, tooling required for manufacturing, systems and processes to provide a service, etc.)

When a product is launched the *selling price* and *advertising* must be specified.

2.5 Advertising, Media & Awareness

Each product must be advertised so that the potential purchasers are familiar with it. *Awareness* is gained through *Advertising* each product in various *Media*. If insufficient money is spent on advertising, the product's awareness will decline over time. Conversely, adding to an already high advertising budget for a product with high awareness will bring little marginal benefit.

Different media vary in their importance to each segment. For example, one segment may be reached primarily by newspaper advertisements, while another may get its information mainly from the internet. Your advertising budget for a product must be allocated to the various media, depending on where your target segment(s) get their information.

2.6 Sales Force & Channels

A product is sold through direct or indirect *Channels* (e.g. specialty shops, direct over the internet, etc.). Each channel takes a certain sales margin which must be considered, along with the cost of manufacturing, when setting the sales price. The same channels serve both markets.

2.7 Units for Attributes

In several places in SABRE, the information presented regarding perceived product attributes is provided on a standard scale, from -25 to +25. This provides a common basis for comparing different attributes, which have very different units of measurement. It also reflects the real world challenges in understanding consumers' perceptions of products, and the fact that there is often a difference between technical specifications and consumer perceptions.

Should you need to convert between the +/-25 non-dimensional units and the actual values, you can use the minimum and maximum values for each attributes range, found in several reports, and equate them to -25 and +25 respectively.

For example, suppose an attribute called "Power" has a range from 10 Watts to 50 Watts. The non-dimensional value of -25 corresponds to 10 Watts, and the non-dimensional value of +25 corresponds to 50 Watts. Linear interpolation between these values is required for converting other values. For example a "0" corresponds to 30 Watts, and "10" corresponds to 38 Watts.

2.8   Summary

For a product to do well in a market it should:
- Have *Attributes* that closely match the *Ideal Points* for one or more *Segments*.
- Have good *Awareness*, leading to predisposition to purchase.
- Have an effective *Sales Force / Channel* strategy.
- Have enough *Product* available to meet demand.

If your product has low market share, it almost certainly is lacking in one or more of these requirements. Furthermore, your company can only do well if your products are profitable, which requires management of the cost of manufacturing, the selling price, and the margins your sales channels take.

3.0   Getting Started with SABRE

3.1   Installation

SABRE is distributed by a self-extracting installation file. To install SABRE, run (double-click on) the self-installing package called "sabre3221partic_setup.exe" (or a similar file name) and follow the instructions.

The minimum requirements for SABRE are: Microsoft Windows 2000 or later, 96 MB of memory, 1024x768, 256 colors, and 30MB of free disk space.

Once it is installed, you may launch SABRE from the icon that is either on your desktop or in your Start Menu under "Programs". SABRE can be uninstalled by using the Add/Remove Programs feature of the Windows Control Panel.

As you read through this document, you may wish to have SABRE running using the sample data (described in the next section) so you can experiment with the features being described.

3.2   Operation

Each period of the simulation is run following this sequence of steps:

1. The administrator writes "results" data files for each team, and distributes the results files to the teams.
2. The teams load the results into SABRE and enter their decisions.
3. The teams' decision files are returned to the administrator, either by a USB flash drive, e-mail, or via a network.
4. The simulation is run out to the next period and each company's performance is calculated.

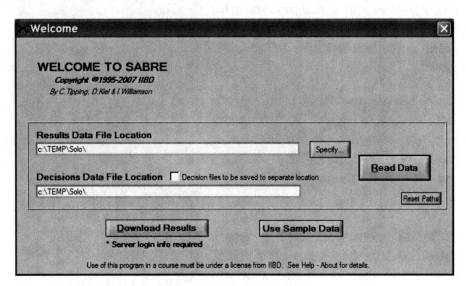

Figure 1 Welcome Screen

When you first use SABRE, a window similar to that shown in Figure 1 is displayed. To get started, SABRE needs to be told where the data files *from* the administrator ("results") are stored on your computer, and where it is to store the data file containing your decisions that will be returned *to* the administrator ("decisions").

In most cases these locations are the same; however, in certain network implementations they may need to be different. To specify a different location for the decision files, click the white check-box.

When SABRE is started, any previously specified results and decisions file locations will be retained. To reset them to the defaults, there is a "Reset Paths" button.

For some simulations you may use SABRE to directly download your results data file and upload your decisions. Detailed instructions for upload and download, including server logon information will be provided by your course administrator. If your simulation does use the upload/download capabilities, the files are still saved locally to enable subsequent off-line use of SABRE.

If you do not yet have a results data file from your course administrator, you may click on "Use Sample Data" to become more familiar with SABRE before your simulation starts.

If you choose to use the sample data, skip to Section 4 ("Accessing Information in SABRE") of this document. When you actually use data from your administrator, you should return to this page for further details on data files.

Before proceeding, you should know where SABRE will be reading results from and where the decision data files should be saved. Your course administrator likely will recommend a standard location that is appropriate for your situation. *It is highly recommended that you start with an empty folder that is dedicated for this purpose.* SABRE defaults to a folder called "..\My Documents\SABRE".

Your administrator will provide you with your data files and a team password. To help avoid any confusion with data files, do not share your password with any competitors. Once you have ensured your files are in the specified location, click on "Read Data".

If there are multiple files for different teams and/or industries in the specified results folder, SABRE will present all the available files for you to select one. SABRE only shows the most recent period's results file for each company to minimize the number of choices.

Next, SABRE will prompt you for your team password. In the first period you may also be prompted for a company name. (Some simulations are set up with fixed names for each team.) At this point, you should enter a name that you want your team to be known by for the rest of the simulation.

File names and locations

Every simulation has a name (or "run name"). If your administrator is running multiple simulations in parallel, each simulation may be referred to as an "industry".

The "run name" or "industry" forms the basis of all file names associated with the simulation. The most important of these are the results and decision data files. The results files all end in .res and the decision files all end in .dec.

To distinguish between files for a particular company or period, the file names include "_C#P#". For example, the results file for Company 3 to use when making decisions for period 4 would be "industry_C3P4.res", and once they have saved their period 4 decisions, the data file containing those decisions would be "industry_C3P4.dec". In this example the name of the simulation is "industry". The "_C#P#" part of the file name is used to identify the results file, so do not rename the results files.

In addition to the decision data file (.dec), a text file (.txt) containing the decision summary report is saved in the same location. This text file is not used by SABRE – it is there only in case you want to quickly double-check your decision file.

If you think you have lost your decision file, for example due to a faulty removable disk, there is one backup location where you can go to recover it. Use Windows Explorer to navigate to either the "Application Data" folder, or the location where the SABRE executable is stored (usually C:\Program Files\IIBD\SABRE\ or similar). From this location there is a folder called DecBackup where you should find a backup of your most recent decisions.

4.0 Accessing Market Information in SABRE

Once it has read in your results files, you will see that SABRE's interface is divided into sections using tabs. At almost any point while using SABRE, you can switch to another tab to view or enter information, and then return to the tab you were previously viewing.

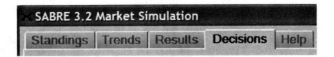

Figure 2: Tabs

Each of the Tabs is described in detail in the following sections.

4.1   Standings Tab

The Standings tab shows plots that compare team performance related to the other teams in the simulation. They are primarily for interest and are not central to the making of business decisions when running your company.

4.2   Trends Tab

The Trends tab shows plots of a variety of values over time for each market or segment. The type of plots available in the top pull-down box will vary from simulation to simulation. You may also select the particular segment or market to plot using the controls on the left. Like the Standing plots, the plots on the Trends tab are available to all teams and do not need to be purchased.

Once one of the controls for the plot, market or segment has been used, a light grey box around its label will identify it as the active control. At this point you may use the up/down arrow keys on your keyboard to scroll through the choices in that control. This is applicable to most controls in SABRE.

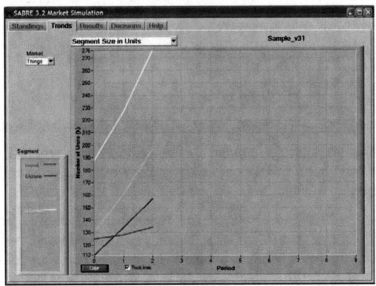

Figure 3: Trends

4.3   Results

The Results tab provides access to the *Reports*, which are generated each period, and the *Studies* which must be purchased. Further details on them are provided in Section 5.4. The report or study can be selected from the list in the left pane and it will be displayed in the right pane.

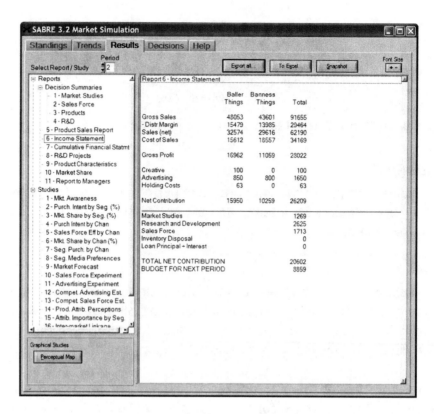

Figure 4: Reports & Studies

The graphical studies (Perceptual Map and Conjoint Study) are accessed with the buttons in the lower left.

There are several features that you may find useful when viewing the results tab:

- The font size can be adjusted with the "+/-" button in the top right.

- The border between the report/study list and the text can be dragged left or right.

- Frequently-used reports or studies can be captured in a separate resizable window using the "Snapshot" button. This can be particularly useful if you have multiple monitors or a large monitor.

- The "Export all" button allows all the reports and studies to be exported to text file, Microsoft Word, or Excel 97 or later. There, you may re-format, re-size, print, or re-arrange them as you see fit. If SABRE is unable to locate Word on your computer, it will ask you to assist in finding it. When exporting data to Word it takes about 10 seconds to prepare Word for the data exchange. Also, please do not operate your PC during the data exchange.

- The "To Excel" button exports just the currently displayed report or study to Excel. Only the text / numeric studies are exported to Excel. The Conjoint and Perceptual Map studies are highly interactive and must be viewed in SABRE.

- As with any Windows program, the image of the current window may be captured to the clipboard by pressing <Alt>-<Print Screen>. The image can then be pasted into any application such as Word, Excel, PowerPoint, an e-mail message, or a graphics program. This can be used to create a custom collection of your important graphs.

4.4   Decisions

All the company decisions are entered within the Decision tab. Note that you can almost always jump to another tab or window while in the middle of entering decisions, and return to finish the data entry.

The details of the Decision tab are covered in section 5.

4.5   Help

The Help tab contains information on file locations, versions, etc. and also the BCG Portfolio plotting tool. The only way to change the file locations is from the initial "Welcome" screen.

5.0   Making Decisions for your Company

Now we can turn to the real focus of the simulation – making decisions. In managing a company in a SABRE simulation, you are required to make decisions in four key areas:

Sales Force
1. How many sales people should you allocate to each channel?
2. How much should you spend on sales force training?

Product Planning
1. Which products should be placed in the marketplace for sale?
2. How much product should be produced to satisfy customer demand?
3. At what price will each product be sold?
4. What should be the quality and quantity of advertising?
5. How should you distribute the advertising budget among the various media?
6. How and where should you best position product offerings?

Market Research (Studies)
1. Reports are free, but which studies should you purchase?
2. How much information is needed in order to make good decisions?

R&D Projects
1. How much should you invest and into which projects?
2. What segments should the development efforts target?
3. What characteristics will be best for the market, given the trends?

Having entered your password (and, if given the opportunity, a team name) you will be presented with the main decision panel which is shown in Figure 5. From here, click on the buttons in the "Enter Decisions" region to make decisions in each of the four key areas for each market.

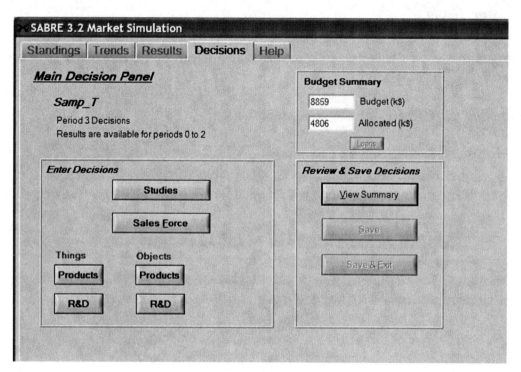

Figure 5: Decision Panel

In the lower half, two columns of buttons correspond to the two markets that are named above them ("Things" and "Objects" in this case). Each button will change color when it is clicked on, to help you keep track of the areas that still need your attention. If you do not specify a new decision on a particular issue, it will default to the same values and selections as in the previous period.

When you have finished making your decisions, click on the "Save Decisions and Exit" button. If, after saving and exiting, you decide that you need to go back and change a decision, start SABRE and click on the "Read Data" button. It will find your results data file and your decision file and ask you if you would like to re-load the decisions.

Note that once you submit your decision file to your administrator, you may not be able to change it. Your administrator will advise you on the policy in place for your simulation.

It is important that as a team you have a system to ensure that all your decisions are recorded in the one file that is submitted. In the main menu under "Output", you can export a text "Decision Summary" that is quite useful for reviewing or sharing with teammates. Note that this text file _is not_ the decision data file that the course administrator requires! The decision data file ends in ".dec" as described in the side-bar in Section 3.

The following is a description of the four main decision areas:

www.iibd.com   +1 250-595-8440   info@iibd.com

5.1   Sales Force

After clicking on a Sales Force button you can set the number of sales staff and the budget for training them. Extra costs are associated with hiring and laying-off sales people, but sales people are transferable between markets, so it is only the *net* change in staff which incurs these hiring and layoff costs.

Figure 6 shows the panel for making Sales Force decisions. You can type in the numbers in the white boxes or click on the increment/decrement arrows. *Yellow* boxes are for information display only; *white* boxes require your input. This color convention applies to all SABRE panels.

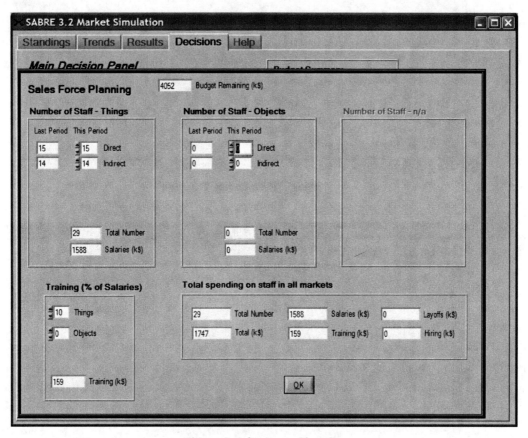

Figure 6: Sales Force Planning

5.2   Products

Products are launched and managed from the "Production Planning" window (shown below in Figure 7) that appears when a "Products" button is clicked in the panel in Figure 5. In each period, you should review your production, pricing and advertising for each product.

By selecting a product in the white box (Figure 7), a summary appears at the bottom. Double-clicking on the product allows you to edit the parameters for that product in the panel shown in Figure 8.

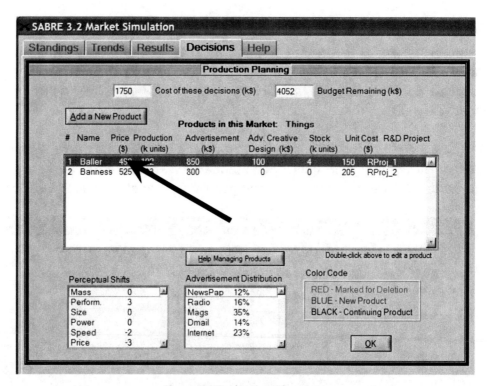

Figure 7: Production Planning

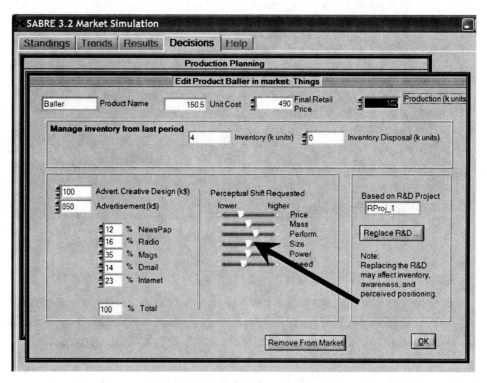

Figure 8: Decisions for a Product

There is a limit to the total number of products (across all markets) that you may have for sale at any given time. Your course instructor will inform you of the actual limit for your simulation. Typically it is between 5 and 10.

Should you need to remove a product from the market, double click on it and select "Remove From Market". It will now appear in red in the list of products. The decision to remove it is final only after you submit your decisions. If you change your mind, it can be returned to the market by double-clicking on it and selecting "Return To Market", but you will need to re-enter decisions for that product.

When making decisions for a product, there are several areas that must be addressed:

Production

When you specify a production number, there is usually a range of plus or minus 15% (your course administrator may inform you of a different value for this) within which your production is adjusted in response to the demand when the simulation is run.

For example, if demand for your product is much lower than you expected, production will be dropped to as low as 85% of your request. If it is far higher, production will be increased up to 115%. Beyond these ranges, you will either be left with extra product in stock to sell next period, or be left with no stock and lost market share. Within these ranges, production will be matched to sales.

Your team must make a trade-off between possible lost sales versus the risk of incurring inventory holding costs. This is a strategic decision and miscalculations can be costly.

Disposal

If you have inventory left from the previous period, and you do not produce any more this period, you may dispose of some of your inventory. This would be done to reduce holding costs in future periods if you expect that your current inventory will not all be sold over the longer term. Your administrator can inform you of the costs associated with disposal in your simulation. Typically they are 10% to 30% of the cost of manufacturing. (In other words, the manufacturing operations of your company can sell the unwanted products at 70% to 90% of the cost of manufacturing, and they pass the 10% - 30% loss on to your profit center.)

Advertising

The primary purpose of advertising in the simulation is to build or maintain product awareness. Over time, awareness of a product will decline unless it is sufficiently advertised. Awareness will typically plateau at some level below 100%, no matter how much you spend.

Advertising is more effective if a fraction of your advertising budget is spent on *advertising creative design* to design effective ads for your target audience.

Advertising must be directed through the media appropriate to the target segment to be most effective. The sum of the percentages directed at each medium, for each product, must be 100%.

Perceptual Shifts

In some simulations, particularly those modeling a consumer market, advertising also has an important role in *Perceptual Shifts*. This allows you to change the way a product is seen by the market. It does not change the product itself, nor does it change the ideal value for a segment – just how the purchasers perceive the product.

Recall that a product's R&D project defines its underlying attributes. However, by requesting a perceptual shift and spending money on advertising, a product can be shifted to move closer to a segment's ideal point. To request a perceptual shift, move the slider shown with an arrow in Figure 8 to the right or left for a particular attribute.

The shifts requested are relative to the current perceptions. A move to the right always increases the attribute's perceived value and a move to the left decreases it. (But increases or decreases are not necessarily better! – See section 2.2.) The farther the slider is moved to the right for example, the more the advertising agency will try to convince customers of an increase.

A perceptual shift does not change the importance of an attribute in the purchase decision – only the perception of a product in the eyes of the customers. Furthermore, the all attributes receive equal emphasis in the advertising campaign, so leaving the slider in the center position reinforces the current position on the Perceptual Map with respect to that attribute, whereas moving the slider to the left or right requests a shift with respect to that attribute.

As in the real world, there is some uncertainty about the actual shift that will be achieved in response to the attempt to change perceptions. The amount of shift that you can achieve is limited. Small shifts are relatively easy to accomplish, but large shifts quickly become much more difficult to achieve. Also, if the product already has high awareness, customer perceptions are harder to change.

With experience, you will get a better idea of how much to move the slider for the desired effect. A good starting assumption is that with the maximum requested shift, and fairly low awareness, you will be able to move the product a noticeable distance on the Perceptual Map. However you will not be able to re-position it wherever you like!

Price

As mentioned earlier, the margins and cost of manufacturing should be considered when setting the price. It is also very important to consider the segment ideal points. In other words, lower is not always better because prices that are too low are associated with low quality.

Although the price is much more easily changed than the other attributes, note also that large changes in price (+ or - 30%) are poorly received by the market. If you need to make such large changes in price, you are often better off launching another product, possibly even from the same R&D project, and using advertising to build awareness under a new name.

Launching New Products

The process of launching a product involves clicking on "Add New Product" in Figure 7, and specifying a name, and the R&D Project on which it is based in the panel shown in Figure 9. Next the usual advertising and perceptual shift data must be entered in the panel shown in Figure 8. Note that new products typically suffer from low awareness, and will require more advertising to get them to a level comparable to existing products.

If you need a product with completely different attributes from what you already have, you will first need to complete an appropriate R&D Project. Only when it is complete will you be able to launch the product.

Multiple products may be launched from a single R&D Project. You will need to use perceptual shifts and/or set different prices to make them appear different to the market.

Once a product is launched, its cost of production is based on the R&D Project with which it is associated. However, this cost of production will decrease over time with an experience curve.

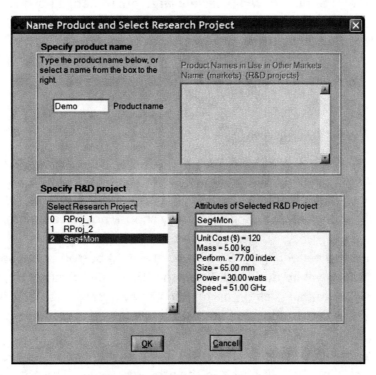

Figure 9: Creating a New Product

It is also important to realize that awareness is associated with the product name. This makes possible more advanced decision-making options: fine-tuning an existing product through R&D, or launching a new product under an old name to capitalize on existing awareness of the old name.

Re-launching Products based on a new R&D Project

In some cases competition or changing needs of a segment will require modifications to a product to reduce the cost of production, or to fine tune some attributes. In this case two options are available: either a new product can be launched, or the existing product can be modified by basing it on a new R&D project.

If a new product is launched, it can be designed to meet the required specifications and the market's perception of it will not be affected by the older product; however, it will initially have low awareness.

If an existing product is modified (i.e. based on a new R&D project) it will benefit from the awareness of that product name, but the market's perception of it may lag behind the actual changes in the product's attributes.

To take the latter approach (base an existing product on a new R&D project), in effect the product must be removed from the market and a new product with exactly the same name is launched based on the newly completed R&D project. This process is achieved by using the "Replace R&D" button on the right side of the window in Figure 8.

As mentioned earlier, the market will receive a large price change poorly, so if you need to change the price by more than about 30%, this procedure is not recommended. In that case, you will generally be better off building a new product name's awareness.

R&D projects that are very similar to previously completed ones are less costly than the original R&D project.

5.3   Research and Development

To create new products that meet the needs of the changing market, you will need to complete R&D Projects. Products may be launched only after the R&D Projects are completed. If you have sufficient funds, you may complete the R&D in one period; however, you may also fund it over several periods. If circumstances change, you may choose not to complete an R&D project.

From the main decision panel (Figure 5), click on the R&D button corresponding to the market for which the R&D project will be designed. From the R&D panel (Figure 10), you can use the button add a new project, or double-click on an ongoing or new project to edit it. The ongoing projects (those initiated in previous periods and not yet complete), can only have their funding adjusted.

When you start a new R&D Project (Figure 10) it is important to be sure to set all the parameters for that project, including the unit cost and the attribute values. The attribute values default to the mid-point of the range for each attribute. To use an existing R&D project's values as the defaults for the new project, <Shift>-double-click on an existing project, or select an existing project and press <Shift><Enter>.

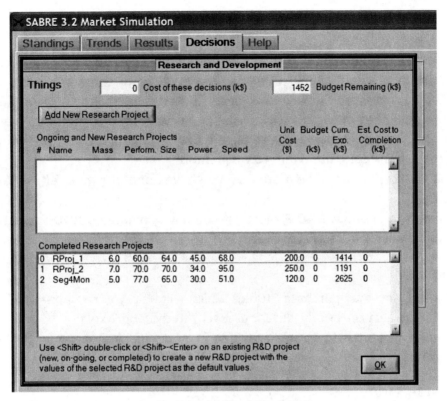

Figure 10: Managing R&D Projects

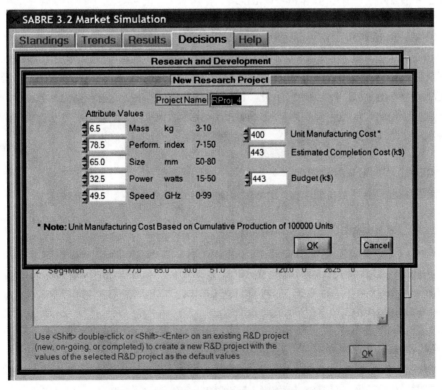

Figure 11: Designing a New R&D Project

There are several factors that contribute to your R&D costs, including:

- Unit cost of production. The lower the production cost, the more the R&D Project will cost.
- The attribute values specified. If the design values of some attributes are set higher, the R&D may cost more; however, other attributes may result in a lower R&D cost if they are increased. For example, the R&D costs for a new notebook computer would be expected to increase if the computer were to have more computing power, but would be expected to decrease if the computer were to weigh more.
- Total R&D experience. The more R&D you have done, the more efficient your company will be at R&D.
- Similarity to previous R&D Projects. If you have completed R&D Projects with very similar attribute values, R&D will cost less.

5.4   Studies

For each market, you may purchase Studies which will help you to understand various aspects of that market. This section briefly describes each Study, and explains how to design a Conjoint Study. Examples of Studies 1-15 are provided in Appendix A. The panel for selecting studies is shown in Figure 12.

1. Market awareness

This study lists each product's market awareness for all companies. Without market awareness, products do not sell, as customers are reluctant to buy products with which they are not familiar. Awareness is achieved through advertising.

2. Purchase intent by segment

This study shows what customers *would* have purchased, based solely on how well each product's perceived attributes match each segment's ideal point(s). This study should be used in conjunction with Study 3, Market Share by Segment. Any discrepancy between the two studies would indicate there has been a breakdown in marketing execution. (e.g. product stocked out, lack of effective sales force supporting the channels, etc.)

3. Market share by segment

This study indicates what customers in each segment actually purchased.

4. Purchase intentions by channel

This study reveals purchase intentions by customers in each channel, based on how well a product meets their needs, and their channel purchase preference. It should be used in conjunction with Study 6, Market Share by Channel. Any discrepancy between the two studies would indicate there has been a breakdown in marketing execution.

5. Sales force effectiveness by channel

This study also shows the overall effectiveness of your sales force by channel. Effectiveness is a function of both the size, and the level of training.

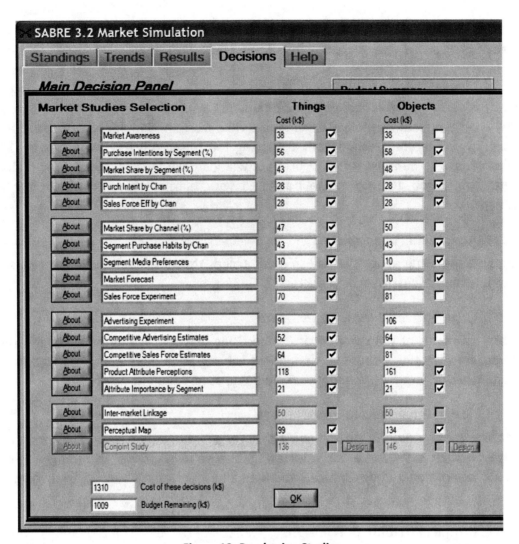

Figure 12: Purchasing Studies

6. Market share by channel

This study shows how much product is actually sold through each channel.

7. Purchase habits by channel

This study shows the market channels through which each segment will purchase.

8. Segment media preferences

This study shows the media sources from which each segment obtains information about the products.

9. Market forecast

This predicts the growth and the size of each market and each segment for the upcoming period. Market dynamics can cause significant discrepancies between predicted market size and actual market size. For example, a product that has stocked out can slow the growth of the market as some consumers will postpone purchasing (causing pent up demand), while others will purchase

www.iibd.com   +1 250-595-8440   info@iibd.com

substitutes. Conversely, if several products are close to the ideal points, the market will grow faster than anticipated, due to the quality of the product offerings.

10. Sales force experiment

This study reports the percent change in demand for all products if you were to increase your sales force by a certain factor (usually 2). Demand differs from market share in that it does not include the effect of you or your competitors producing too few products. Note that a +10% change in demand means the demand for your product will increase by a factor of 1.1. It **does not mean** that you should add 10 percentage points to your market share to obtain the result of the experiment!

11. Advertising experiment

This study is the same as for the Sales Force, except that the Advertising budget is adjusted and the percent change in demand is reported.

12. Competitive advertising estimates

These are estimates of the competitors' advertising levels. Lagging or leading in this area could mean you are investing either not enough or too much in advertising. (Comparing these third party estimates of your own spending can help you assess their accuracy.)

13. Competitive sales force estimates

Like the previous study, this one shows estimates of what other companies are estimated to be spending on their sales force, so you may gauge your response accordingly. This study also includes a performance index which estimates the level of training of each competitor's sales force.

14. Product attribute perceptions

Customers compare all of the products on the market to assess their similarities and differences. This data is used to determine customer perceptions of the products. Each attribute of each product is placed on an arbitrary scale. Are your products perceived as being too fast or too slow in speed? Too high or too low in price? This study will tell you where you are positioned in the purchasers' minds, and what each segment ideally wants. The perceptual map (Study 17) is drawn from these values.

15. Attribute importance by segment

For each segment, this study estimates the importance of each of the attributes in the purchase decision. This information is useful to assess the significance of the distances seen in the Perceptual Map and will help identify which attributes must be correct to meet a segment's needs.

17. Perceptual map

This study plots pairs of attributes on a perceptual map to show each product's perceived position in the marketplace, as seen by the purchasers. An example of the Perceptual Map is shown in Figure 13. The letters on the plot denote products, and the numbers denote the segments.

The Perceptual Map will usually show a cloud of points comprising each segment, indicating the distribution of ideal points within the segment's members.

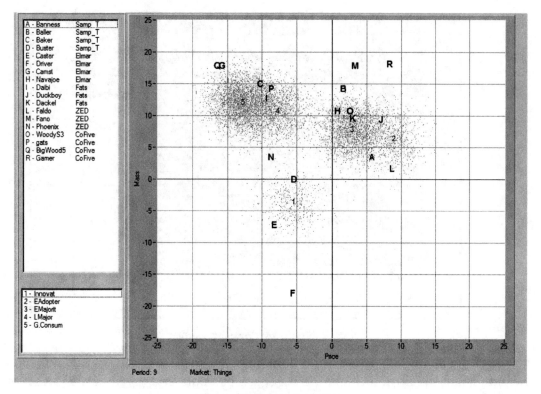

Figure 13: Perceptual Map

18. Conjoint study

SABRE presents results similar to those obtained if a sample of a population of purchasers were presented with a conjoint study. In such a study, the participants are asked to respond to some hypothetical product offerings, typically by scoring, sorting, or selecting from a set of choices. The relative response to the various hypothetical products can then be interpreted to gain significant insight into the respondents' product preferences.

In SABRE, the results are presented on a per-segment basis. In some simulations you are able to set the attribute levels for the study on a per-segment basis. In other simulations, you are restricted to setting a single set of levels per attribute. In the latter case, the study is best used by designing the study to obtain information on the segment of most interest for that attribute. Your administrator may also elect to have SABRE set reasonable default levels each period.

This study plots the relative response of each segment to different levels (i.e. values) of each attribute. The plot is put on a relative scale and reflects (a) the homogeneity or distribution of the members of the segment, (b) the range of levels which the respondents are asked to assess, and (c) the importance of that attribute in their purchase decision. An example is shown in Figure 14.

In this plot, the market, attribute and period can be specified. Each plotted line corresponds to a segment shown in the legend. A plot that rises and then declines indicates that the segment ideal point is somewhere in the middle of the range of levels used. However, a rising or falling plot shows that the segments ideal point is out of the range of attribute levels used in the study.

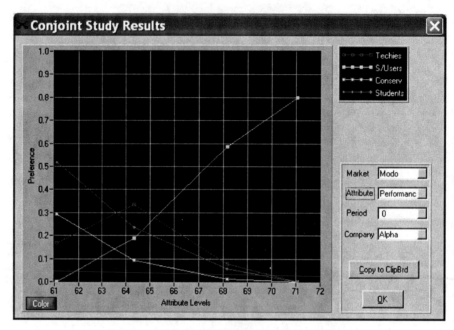

Figure 14: Conjoint Study

The height of the plot is a measure of (a) how close the levels were set to the middle of a segment, (b) how important the attribute is in the purchase decision, and (c) what the lowest response was for that segment. This last point is crucial to properly designing the Conjoint Study. You must select levels that will elicit a wide range of responses from the respondents. In practice, this means keeping at least one of your extreme values near the boundaries or outside the segment's distribution of preferences for that attribute.

In some cases, the plot is flat, or very nearly flat. This can arise if (a) the attribute has negligible importance in the purchase decision, or (b) if the segment is highly heterogeneous in its response to that attribute (i.e. on the Perceptual Map the cloud of points is widely spread) relative to the range of levels used in the study, or (c) the attribute levels are so far from the ideal for that segment that the response is uniformly poor to all the attribute levels used.

In cases (b) and (c) above, the design of the conjoint study levels for that attribute can be improved for that segment.

As mentioned earlier, to design an effective conjoint study, you must select levels that are close enough to the segment ideal point to obtain a positive response. You must also set other levels that are sufficiently different so as to obtain a range of responses. The minimum and maximum responses are used to scale the final results.

To design a conjoint study, click on the "Design Conjoint" button on the Market Studies decision panel (Figure 12). This will bring up a panel that shows a tabular summary of your conjoint design (Figure 15). In some simulations, you must set the levels for each segment while, for others, only one set of levels is available. If the "Segment" box is not grayed-out, you must use it to set levels for each segment. If you do not set conjoint levels for a period, the values default to those in the previous period.

To set the levels:
1. Click on an attribute in the main white box. It will be highlighted in blue.
2. Use the four white boxes below to set the attribute levels, either by typing in values or using the increment/decrement arrows.
3. The new levels are indicated with vertical red lines on the graph to the right. If you bought the conjoint study in the previous period, the results are plotted for comparison.
4. Repeat steps 1-3 for all attributes.
5. If available, select the next segment, and repeat steps 1-4.

While making these changes, the plot on the right displays the current attribute Conjoint Results for the last period (if purchased) and a red vertical line to show the new levels being set.

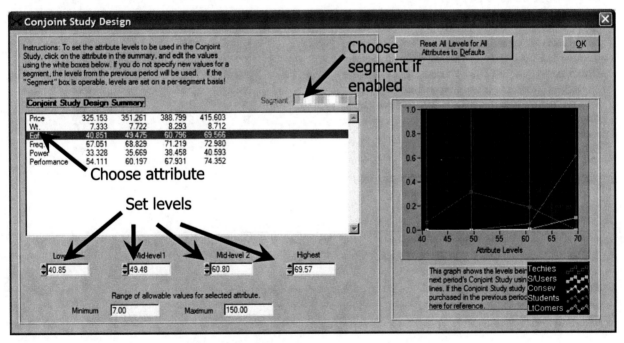

Figure 15: Designing Next Period's Conjoint Study

6.0   Conclusion

You now have the information needed to compete and be successful in SABRE. If you have difficulties that can not be resolved using this guide, please consult your course administrator. Good luck and have fun!

Appendix A – Sample Reports and Studies

REPORT 1: DECISION SUMMARY - MARKET STUDIES

Run Name: Sample_v31
Company: Samp_T (Company 1)
Period: 2

	Things		Objects	
	Y/N	(k$)	Y/N	(k$)
Market Awareness	Y	36	N	36
Purchase Intentions by Segment (%)	Y	54	Y	56
Market Share by Segment (%)	Y	42	N	47
Purch Intent by Chan	Y	27	Y	27
Sales Force Eff by Chan	Y	27	Y	27
Market Share by Channel (%)	Y	46	N	49
Segment Purchase Habits by Chan	Y	42	Y	42
Segment Media Preferences	Y	9	Y	9
Market Forecast	Y	9	Y	9
Sales Force Experiment	Y	68	N	78
Advertising Experiment	Y	88	N	103
Competitive Advertising Estimates	Y	50	N	62
Competitive Sales Force Estimates	Y	62	N	78
Product Attribute Perceptions	Y	114	Y	156
Attribute Importance by Segment	Y	21	Y	21
Inter-market Linkage	N	50	N	50
Perceptual Map	Y	96	Y	130
Conjoint Study	N	132	N	141

TOTAL EXPENDITURE ON STUDIES (k$)   1269

REPORT 2: DECISION SUMMARY - SALES FORCE

Run Name: Sample_v31
Company: Samp_T (Company 1)
Period: 2

Number of Sales Personnel

Channel	Direct	Indirect	Train.%
Market: Things	15	14	10
Market: Objects	0	0	0

Expenditure on Training (k$)	154
Expenditure on Salaries (k$)	1539
Expenditure on Hiring (k$)	21
Expenditure on Layoffs (k$)	0

TOTAL SALES FORCE EXPENDITURES (k$)   1713

REPORT 3: DECISION SUMMARY - PRODUCTION

Run Name: Sample_v31
Company: Samp_T (Company 1)
Period: 2

Products	Baller	Banness
Research Project	RProj_1	RProj_2
Market	Things	Things
Sale Price ($)	490.0	525.0
Production (k)	120	75
Disposal (k)	0	0
Creative Des(k$)	100	0
Advertising (k$)	850	800

Advertisement Channels

NewsPap (%)	12	25
Radio (%)	16	10
Mags (%)	35	30
Dmail (%)	14	5
Internet (%)	23	30

Perceptual Shifts

Price	0	-4
Mass/Rating	0	0
Perform./Length	1	4
Size/Battery	0	0
Power/Weight	0	0
Speed/Ease	2	0

TOTAL ADVERTISEMENT EXPENSES (k$)   1750

REPORT 4: DECISION SUMMARY - RESEARCH & DEVELOPMENT PROJECTS

Run Name: Sample_v31
Company: Samp_T (Company 1)
Period: 2

Market: Things

	Mass kg 3-10	Perform. index 7-150	Size mm 50-80	Power watts 15-50	Speed GHz 0-99	Unit Cost ($)	Budget (k$)
Project							
Seg4Mon	5	77	65	30	51	120.0	2625

Market: Objects

	Rating index 7-15	Length cm 50-95	Battery hours 1-6	Weight grams 100-900	Ease index 0-99	Unit Cost ($)	Budget (k$)
Project							

TOTAL RESEARCH AND DEVELOPMENT EXPENDITURES (k$)   2625

SUMMARY

Available Budget (k$)	8080
Committed Budget (k$)	7357
Loans (k$)	0
Inventory Disposal (k$)	0
TOTAL COMMITMENT (k$)	7357

REPORT 5: PRODUCT SALES REPORT

Run Name: Sample_v31
Company: Samp_T (Company 1)
Period: 2

Market	Baller Things	Banness Things	Total
R&D Project	RProj_1	RProj_2	
Retail Price $	490	525	
Unit Cost $	159	223	
Ini. Inventory k	0	0	
Requested k	120	75	195
Disposal k	0	0	
Produced k	102	83	185
Sold k	98	83	181
Fin. Inventory k	4	0	4

REPORT 6: INCOME STATEMENT (k$)

Run Name: Sample_v31
Company: Samp_T (Company 1)
Period: 2

	Baller Things	Banness Things	Total
Gross Sales	48053	43601	91655
- Distr Margin	15479	13985	29464
Sales (net)	32574	29616	62190
Cost of Sales	15612	18557	34169
Gross Profit	16962	11059	28022
Advertising	950	800	1750
Holding Costs	63	0	63
Net Contribution	15950	10259	26209

Market Studies	1269
Research and Development	2625
Sales Force	1713
Inventory Disposal	0
Loan Principal + Interest	0
TOTAL NET CONTRIBUTION	20602
BUDGET FOR NEXT PERIOD	8859

REPORT 7: CUMULATIVE FINANCIAL STATEMENT (k$)

Run Name: Sample_v31
Company: Samp_T (Company 1)
Period: 2

Total Sales Revenue	139410
Cost of Sales	81820
Gross Profit	57590

Less Expenses

Advertising Expenses	6160
Market Studies	2799
Research and Development	2625
Sales Force	4303

Less Other Expenses

Inventory Holding Costs	2533
Inventory Disposal Costs	0
Loan Principal + Interest	0

Total expenses	18419

TOTAL CUMULATIVE NET CONTRIBUTION	85454

REPORT 8: RESEARCH AND DEVELOPMENT PROJECTS

Run Name: Sample_v31
Company: Samp_T (Company 1)
Period: 2

Things
    Successful Projects

	Mass kg 3-10	Perform. index 7-150	Size mm 50-80	Power watts 15-50	Speed GHz 0-99	Unit Cost ($)	Amount Spent (k$)
RProj_1	6	60	64	45	68	200.0	1414
RProj_2	7	70	70	34	95	250.0	1191
Seg4Mon	5	77	65	30	51	120.0	2625

    Incomplete Projects

** NOTE: Unit Manufacturing Cost Based on the Production of 100000 Units

---

Objects
    Successful Projects

Rating index 7-15	Length cm 50-95	Battery hours 1-6	Weight grams 100-900	Ease index 0-99	Unit Cost ($)	Amount Spent (k$)

    Incomplete Projects

** NOTE: Unit Manufacturing Cost Based on the Production of 100000 Units

---

REPORT 9: PRODUCT CHARACTERISTICS

Run Name: Sample_v31
Company: Samp_T (Company 1)
Period: 2

Things

	Mass kg 3-10	Perform. index 7-150	Size mm 50-80	Power watts 15-50	Speed GHz 0-99	Unit Cost ($)	Sales Price ($)
Samp_T							
Baller	6	60	64	45	68	200	490
Banness	7	70	70	34	95	250	525
Elmar							
Caster	7	66	55	35	27	119	275
Camst	6	56	76	29	22	112	250
Fanatics							
Danil	4	58	78	45	27	117	263
Daibi	5	48	57	25	24	112	279
ZED							
Faldo	7	35	67	40	75	210	368
Fano	5	33	55	25	90	240	480
CoFive							
Gats	8	141	75	41	16	120	285
Gamer	5	29	78	41	72	215	470

Objects

Rating index 7-15	Length cm 50-95	Battery hours 1-6	Weight grams 100-900	Ease index 0-99	Unit Cost ($)	Sales Price ($)

REPORT 10: MARKET SHARE

Run Name: Sample_v31
Company: Samp_T (Company 1)
Period: 2

Things

	% Market Share (units)	% Market Share (value)
Samp_T		
Baller	9.9	13.8
Banness	8.4	12.6
Elmar		
Caster	14.1	10.8
Camst	11.9	8.4
Fanatics		
Danil	13.7	10.1
Daibi	10.9	8.5
ZED		
Faldo	8.2	8.6
Fano	7.9	10.8
CoFive		
Gats	7.3	5.9
Gamer	7.7	10.3

TOTAL UNITS SOLD (k)   989
TOTAL MARKET VALUE (k$)   348930

Objects

	% Market Share (units)	% Market Share (value)
TOTAL UNITS SOLD (k)	0	
TOTAL MARKET VALUE (k$)	0	

REPORT 11: REPORT TO MANAGERS

Run Name: Sample_v31
Company: Samp_T (Company 1)
Period: 2

Next Period Forecast

```
Economic growth (%)...........................................    5.4
Inflation (%) ................................................    3.2
Cost to carry inventory (% of Unit Cost) .....................   10.0
Cost of inventory liquidation (% of Unit Cost)................   10.0
Salaries (per annum) .........................................  54752
Channel Margin (%) -                    Direct                    30
Channel Margin (%) -                    Indirect                  35
```

Detailed Sales Force Report

Things

	Training(%)	Tot.#	Hires	Xfers
Previous period	12	25	0	0
This period	10	29	0	0

Effectiveness

	Direct	Indirect
Previous period	0.82	0.73
This period	0.75	0.72

Objects

	Training(%)	Tot.#	Hires	Xfers
Previous period	0	0	-	-
This period	0	0	-	-

Effectiveness

	Direct	Indirect
Previous period		
This period	-	-

Market Study 1: Market Awareness

Run Name: Sample_v3
Market: Things
Company: Samp_T (Company1)
Period: 2

Company	Product	Innovat	EAdopter	EMajorit	LMajor	G.Consum
Samp_T	A Baller	0.69	0.69	0.69	0.69	0.69
	B Banness	0.71	0.71	0.71	0.71	0.71
Elmar	C Caster	0.79	0.79	0.79	0.79	0.79
	D Camst	0.79	0.79	0.79	0.79	0.79
Fanatics	E Danil	0.76	0.76	0.76	0.76	0.76
	F Daibi	0.79	0.79	0.79	0.79	0.79
ZED	G Faldo	0.71	0.71	0.71	0.71	0.71
	H Fano	0.79	0.79	0.79	0.79	0.79
CoFive	I Gats	0.80	0.80	0.80	0.80	0.80
	J Gamer	0.80	0.80	0.80	0.80	0.80

Market Study 2: Purchase Intentions by Segment (%)

Run Name: Sample_v3
Market: Things
Company: Samp_T (Company1)
Period: 2

Company	Product	Innovat	EAdopter	EMajorit	LMajor	G.Consum	Overall
Samp_T	A Baller	11.7	15.8	16.5	10.4	4.7	11.2
	B Banness	12.9	16.1	11.4	7.3	3.4	9.3
Elmar	C Caster	10.0	8.8	10.5	15.6	20.3	13.9
	D Camst	8.8	7.5	8.6	11.4	18.7	11.8
Fanatics	E Danil	9.7	8.3	9.7	14.2	21.6	13.7
	F Daibi	8.6	7.5	8.7	10.8	14.5	10.6
ZED	G Faldo	10.3	10.1	9.5	9.2	4.5	8.3
	H Fano	9.1	9.4	8.5	6.6	3.4	6.9
CoFive	I Gats	10.1	7.1	7.4	7.0	5.0	7.0
	J Gamer	8.8	9.3	9.2	7.4	4.0	7.3

Market Study 3: Market Share by Segment (%)

Run Name: Sample_v3
Market: Things
Company: Samp_T (Company1)
Period: 2

Company	Product	Innovat	EAdopter	EMajorit	LMajor	G.Consum	Total
Samp_T	A Baller	10.6	14.2	14.8	9.0	3.8	9.9
	B Banness	11.8	14.7	10.5	6.4	2.8	8.4
Elmar	C Caster	9.0	8.6	10.1	16.4	21.2	14.1
	D Camst	7.9	7.3	8.3	12.0	19.5	11.9
Fanatics	E Danil	9.0	8.2	9.6	14.6	21.8	13.7
	F Daibi	8.3	7.6	8.9	11.5	15.2	10.9
ZED	G Faldo	11.5	10.6	10.0	8.3	3.7	8.2
	H Fano	11.6	11.2	10.1	6.7	3.2	7.9
CoFive	I Gats	10.8	7.6	7.9	7.3	4.9	7.3
	J Gamer	9.4	10.0	9.9	7.7	3.9	7.7

Market Study 4: Purch Intent by Chan

Run Name: Sample_v3
Market: Things
Company: Samp_T (Company1)
Period: 2

Company	Product	Direct	Indirect	Total
Samp_T	A Baller	13.4	9.4	11.2
	B Banness	11.7	7.3	9.3
Elmar	C Caster	11.4	16.0	13.9
	D Camst	9.5	13.7	11.8
Fanatics	E Danil	10.9	16.0	13.7
	F Daibi	9.1	11.7	10.6
ZED	G Faldo	9.4	7.3	8.3
	H Fano	8.2	5.9	6.9
CoFive	I Gats	7.8	6.3	7.0
	J Gamer	8.5	6.4	7.3

Market Study 5: Sales Force Eff by Chan

Run Name: Sample_v3
Market: Things
Company: Samp_T (Company1)
Period: 2

Sales Force Effectiveness by Channel (0-1)

Company	Direct	Indirect
Samp_T	0.75	0.72
Elmar	0.60	0.82
Fanatics	0.67	0.82
ZED	0.95	0.66
CoFive	0.75	0.74

Market Study 6: Market Share by Channel (%)

Run Name: Sample_v3
Market: Things
Company: Samp_T (Company1)
Period: 2

Company	Product	Direct	Indirect	Total
Samp_T	A Baller	12.3	8.0	9.9
	B Banness	10.9	6.3	8.4
Elmar	C Caster	9.9	17.5	14.1
	D Camst	8.3	15.0	11.9
Fanatics	E Danil	10.0	16.7	13.7
	F Daibi	8.7	12.7	10.9
ZED	G Faldo	11.2	5.7	8.2
	H Fano	11.1	5.2	7.9
CoFive	I Gats	8.5	6.4	7.3
	J Gamer	9.2	6.5	7.7

www.iibd.com   +1 250-595-8440   info@iibd.com

Market Study 7: Segment Purchase Habits by Chan

Run Name: Sample_v3
Market: Things
Company: Samp_T (Company1)
Period: 2

	Innovat	EAdopter	EMajorit	LMajor	G.Consum
Purchase Habits					
Direct	85.4	63.8	62.6	27.3	12.9
Indirect	14.6	36.2	37.4	72.7	87.1

Market Study 8: Segment Media Preferences

Run Name: Sample_v3
Market: Things
Company: Samp_T (Company1)
Period: 2

	Innovat	EAdopter	EMajorit	LMajor	G.Consum
Information Sources					
NewsPap	20.0	20.0	20.0	20.0	20.0
Radio	20.0	20.0	20.0	20.0	20.0
Mags	20.0	20.0	20.0	20.0	20.0
Dmail	20.0	20.0	20.0	20.0	20.0
Internet	20.0	20.0	20.0	20.0	20.0

Market Study 9: Market Forecast

Run Name: Sample_v3
Market: Things
Company: Samp_T (Company 1)
Period: 2

Segment	Current Units (k)	Projected Growth (%)	Projected Units (k)
Innovat	135	3	139
EAdopter	157	15	181
EMajorit	223	23	275
LMajor	197	23	243
G.Consum	276	24	343
Total	989	19	1180

Note: In markets with no sales, numbers reflect potential market size.

Market Study 10: Sales Force Experiment

Run Name: Sample_v3
Market: Things
Company: Samp_T (Company1)
Period: 2

Company	Product	Innovat	EAdopter	EMajorit	LMajor	G.Consum	Total
Samp_T	A Baller	+19%	+17%	+18%	+22%	+25%	+19%
	B Banness	+19%	+17%	+18%	+22%	+25%	+19%
Elmar	C Caster	-2%	-5%	-4%	-3%	-1%	-2%
	D Camst	-2%	-5%	-4%	-3%	-1%	-2%
Fanatics	E Danil	-4%	-6%	-5%	-3%	-1%	-3%
	F Daibi	-4%	-6%	-5%	-3%	-1%	-3%
ZED	G Faldo	-5%	-6%	-5%	-2%	+0%	-4%
	H Fano	-5%	-6%	-5%	-2%	+0%	-4%
CoFive	I Gats	-6%	-7%	-6%	-3%	-1%	-5%
	J Gamer	-6%	-7%	-6%	-3%	-1%	-5%

Percent change in demand if your Sales Force were multiplied by 2.0

(For example +100 means that twice as many purchasers would want to buy the product, if everything else including competitors' actions were held constant. Note that stock-outs can prevent demand from being met.)

Market Study 11: Advertising Experiment

Run Name: Sample_v3
Market: Things
Company: Samp_T (Company1)Administrator
Period: 2

Company	Product	Innovat	EAdopter	EMajorit	LMajor	G.Consum	Total
Samp_T	A Baller	+15%	+13%	+14%	+16%	+18%	+15%
	B Banness	+12%	+11%	+11%	+13%	+15%	+12%
Elmar	C Caster	-3%	-4%	-3%	-1%	+0%	-1%
	D Camst	-3%	-4%	-3%	-1%	+0%	-1%
Fanatics	E Danil	-3%	-4%	-4%	-2%	-1%	-2%
	F Daibi	-3%	-4%	-4%	-2%	+0%	-2%
ZED	G Faldo	-3%	-4%	-4%	-2%	-1%	-3%
	H Fano	-3%	-4%	-4%	-2%	-1%	-3%
CoFive	I Gats	-2%	-3%	-3%	-1%	+0%	-2%
	J Gamer	-2%	-3%	-3%	-1%	+0%	-2%

Percent change in demand if your Advertisement expenditure were multiplied by 2.0

(For example +100 means that twice as many purchasers would want to buy the product, if everything else including competitors' actions were held constant. Note that stock-outs can prevent demand from being met.)

Market Study 12: Competitive Advertising Estimates

Run Name: Sample_v3
Market: Things
Company: Samp_T (Company 1)
Period: 2

Advertising (k$)

Company	Product	NewsPap	Radio	Mags	Dmail	Internet	Total
Samp_T	A Baller	93	146	323	107	256	925
	B Banness	231	86	239	34	242	832
Elmar	C Caster	0	273	446	696	0	1415
	D Camst	0	375	429	536	0	1340
Fanatics	E Danil	109	203	162	299	56	829
	F Daibi	131	196	293	379	77	1076
ZED	G Faldo	0	207	231	217	0	655
	H Fano	116	119	525	254	259	1273
CoFive	I Gats	514	600	182	629	193	2118
	J Gamer	137	176	807	185	442	1747

Market Study 13: Competitive Sales Force Estimates

Run Name: Sample_v3
Market: Things
Company: Samp_T (Company 1)
Period: 2

Company	Direct	Indirect	Total	Performance Index
Samp_T	13	15	28	9.8
Elmar	5	22	27	9.8
Fanatics	10	22	32	10.0
ZED	29	10	39	10.0
CoFive	13	13	26	9.8

Note: Performance Index Range; 0=Poor to 10=Excellent

Market Study 14: Product Attribute Perceptions

Run Name: Sample_v3
Market: Things
Company: Samp_T (Company 1)
Period: 2

Segment Ideal Values (-25 to +25)

	Innovat	EAdopter	EMajorit	LMajor	G.Consum
Price	-8.25	3.92	5.00	-9.25	-14.08
Mass	7.14	15.00	17.14	20.00	20.71
Perform.	16.26	8.57	5.77	1.57	-3.32
Size	6.67	3.33	13.33	2.50	-1.33
Power	-13.14	-19.29	-13.57	-15.00	-16.43
Speed	19.95	12.88	4.29	2.78	-9.85

Product Values (-25 to +25)

Company	Product	Price	Mass	Perform.	Size	Power	Speed
Samp_T	A Baller	5.81	-3.57	-5.41	-1.67	17.86	10.67
	B Banness	8.81	3.57	-1.36	8.33	2.14	22.98
Elmar	C Caster	-8.16	3.57	-4.37	-16.67	3.57	-8.59
	D Camst	-9.51	-3.57	-7.87	18.33	-5.00	-11.96
Fanatics	E Danil	-8.91	-17.86	-4.93	19.71	17.86	-9.58
	F Daibi	-7.40	-10.71	-8.10	-13.33	-10.71	-12.88
ZED	G Faldo	-0.75	3.57	-13.30	3.33	10.71	15.17
	H Fano	8.56	-10.71	-14.02	-16.67	-10.71	20.45
CoFive	I Gats	-9.58	10.71	21.85	16.67	12.14	-16.92
	J Gamer	7.41	-10.71	-15.55	21.67	12.14	12.94

Market Study 15: Attribute Importance by Segment

Run Name: Sample_v3
Market: Things
Company: Samp_T (Company 1)
Period: 2

	Innovat	EAdopter	EMajorit	LMajor	G.Consum
Price	1.0	1.0	1.0	1.0	1.0
Mass	0.2	0.1	0.1	0.1	0.1
Perform.	1.0	1.0	1.0	1.0	1.0
Size	0.0	0.0	0.0	0.0	0.0
Power	0.0	0.0	0.0	0.0	0.0
Speed	0.8	0.9	0.9	0.9	0.9

Note: High = 1; Low = 0

Market Study 17: Perceptual Map

Run Name: Sample_v3
Market: Things
Company: Samp_T (Company1)
Period: 2

A sample of the Perceptual Map is provided in Figure 13

[Note: Perceptual Maps are provided for some or all attributes, depending on the simulation.]

Market Study 18 – Conjoint Study

Run Name: Sample
Market: Things
Period: 9

A sample of the Conjoint Study is provided in Figure 14

H A R V A R D | B U S I N E S S | S C H O O L

9-580-104

REV: AUGUST 16, 1985

BENSON P. SHAPIRO

JEFFREY J. SHERMAN

Cumberland Metal Industries: Engineered Products Division, 1980

Robert Minicucci,[1] vice president of the Engineered Products Division of Cumberland Metal Industries (CMI), and Thomas Simpson, group manager of the Mechanical Products Group, had spent the entire Wednesday (January 2, 1980) reviewing a new product CMI was about to introduce. (See **Exhibit 1** for organization charts.) The room was silent, and as he watched the waning rays of the sun filtering through the window, Minicucci pondered all that had been said. Turning toward Simpson, he paused before speaking.

> Curled metal cushion pads seem to have more potential than any product we've ever introduced. A successful market introduction could as much as double the sales of this company, as well as compensate for the decline of some existing lines. It almost looks too good to be true.

Simpson responded, "The people at Colerick Foundation Company are pressing us to sell to them. Since they did the original test, they've been anxious to buy more. I promised to contact them by the end of the week."

"Fair enough," Minicucci said, "but talk to me before you call them. The way we price this could have a significant impact on everything else we do with it."

The Company

Cumberland Metal Industries was one of the largest manufacturers of curled metal products in the country, having grown from $250,000 in sales in 1963 to over $18,500,000 by 1979. (**Exhibit 2** shows CMI's income statement.) It originally custom fabricated components for chemical process filtration and other highly technical applications. Company philosophy soon evolved from selling the metal as a finished product to selling products that used it as a raw material.

The company's big boost came with the introduction of exhaust gas recirculation (EGR) valves on U.S. automobiles. Both the Ford and Chrysler valve designs required a high temperature seal to hold the elements in place and prevent the escape of very hot exhaust gases. Cumberland developed a product that sold under the trademark *Slip-Seal*. Because it could meet the demanding specifications

---

[1] Pronounced *Minikuchi*.

Professor Benson P. Shapiro and Jeffrey J. Sherman prepared this case. HBS cases are developed solely as the basis for class discussion. It was made possible by a company that prefers to remain anonymous. All data have been disguised. Cases are not intended to serve as endorsements, sources of primary data, or illustrations of effective or ineffective management.

of the automakers, the product captured a very large percentage of the available business, and the company grew quite rapidly through the mid-1970s. Company management was not sanguine about maintaining its 80% market share over the long term, however, and moved to diversify away from a total reliance on the product and industry. Thus, when a sales representative from Houston approached CMI with a new application for curled metal technology, management examined it closely.

The Product

Background

The product that Minicucci and Simpson were talking about was a cushion pad—an integral part of the process for driving piles.[2] Pile driving was generally done with a large crane, to which a diesel or steam hammer inside a set of leads was attached. The leads were suspended over the pile for direction and support. The hammer drove the pile from the top of the leads to a sufficient depth in the ground (see **Exhibit 3**).

The cushion pads prevented the shock of the hammer from damaging hammer or pile. They sat in a circular "helmet" placed over the top of the pile and were stacked to keep air from coming between striker plate and ram, as shown in **Exhibit 3**. Of equal importance, the pads effectively transmitted energy from the hammer to the pile. A good cushion pad had to be able to transmit force without creating heat, and still remain resilient enough to prevent shock. With an ineffective pad, energy transmitted from the hammer would be given off as heat, and the pile could start to vibrate and possibly crack.

Despite the importance of these pads to the pile-driving process, little attention had been paid to them by most of the industry. Originally hardwood blocks had been used. Although their cushioning was adequate, availability was a problem and performance was poor. Constant pounding quickly destroyed the wood's resiliency, heat built up, and the wood often ignited. The blocks had to be replaced frequently.

Most of the industry had shifted to asbestos pads (normally $1/4$-inch thick) which were used most often and seemed to perform adequately, or stacks of alternate layers of $1/2$-inch-thick aluminum plate and 1-inch-thick micarta slabs. (These were not fabricated, but simply pieces of micarta and aluminum cut to specific dimensions.) Both pads came in a variety of standard diameters, the most common being 11 $1/2$ inches. Diameter was determined by the size of the helmet, which varied with the size of the pile.

Curled Metal and the CMI Cushion Pad

Curled metal was a continuous metal wire that had been flattened and then wound into tight, continuous ringlets. These allowed the metal to stretch in both length and width and gave it three-dimensional resiliency. Because it could be made of various metals (such as copper, monel, and stainless steel), curled metal could be made to withstand almost any temperature or chemical. Stacking many layers could produce a shock mount, an airflow corrector or a highly efficient filter. Tightly compressed curled

---

[2] Piles were heavy beams of wood, concrete, steel, or a composite material which were pushed into the ground as support for a building, bridge, or other structure. They were necessary where the geological composition could shift under the weight of an unsupported structure.

metal could produce the Slip-Seal for exhaust systems applications or, when calendered and wound around an axis, a cushion pad for pile driving.[3]

Cumberland purchased the wire from outside vendors and performed the flattening and curling operations in-house. The CMI pad started with curled metal calendered to about one inch thick and wound tightly around the center of a flat, metallic disk until the desired diameter had been reached. A similar disk was placed on top, with soldered tabs folded down to hold it all together. The entire structure was then coated with polyvinyl chloride to enhance its appearance and disguise the contents (see **Exhibit 4**).[4]

The advantage of this manufacturing process was that any diameter pad, from the standard minimum of 11 $1/2$ inches to over 30 inches for a custom-designed application, could be produced from the same band of curled metal.

Comparative Performance

The Colerick Test

After struggling to find a responsible contractor to use the product and monitor its performance, CMI persuaded Colerick Foundation Company of Baltimore, Maryland, to try its pads on a papermill expansion in Newark, Delaware. The job required 300 55-foot piles driven 50 feet into the ground. The piles were 10-inch and 14-inch steel H-beams; both used an 11 ½-inch helmet and, thus, 11 ½-inch cushion pads. The total contractor revenue from the job was $75,000 ($5 per foot of pile driven).

Colerick drove a number of piles using the conventional $1/4$-inch thick asbestos cushion pads to determine their characteristics for the job. Eighteen were placed in the helmet and driven until they lost resiliency. Pads were added, and driving continued until a complete set of 24 were sitting in the helmet. After these were spent, the entire set was removed and the cycle repeated.

The rest of the job used the CMI pads. Four were initially installed and driven until 46 piles had been placed. One pad was added and the driving continued for 184 more piles. Another pad was placed in the helmet, and the job was completed. Comparable performances for the entire job were extrapolated as follows:

		Asbestos	CMI
1.	Feet driven per hour while pile driver was at work (does not consider downtime)	150	200
2.	Piles driven per set of pads	15	300
3.	Number of pads per set	24	6
4.	Number of sets required	20	1
5.	Number of set changes	20	1
6.	Time required for change per set	20 mins.	4 mins.
7.	Colerick cost per set	$50	Not charged

---

[3] In calendering, curled metal ringlets were compressed between rollers to make a smooth, tight band.

[4] The managers at CMI were concerned that other manufacturers might discover this new application for curled metal and enter the business before CMI could get patent protection. The company had a number of competitors, most of whom were substantially smaller than CMI and none of whom had shown a strong interest or competence in technical, market, or product development.

Although the CMI pads drove piles 33% faster than the asbestos and lasted for the entire job, Simpson felt these results were unusual. He believed that a curled metal set life of 10 times more than asbestos and a performance increase of 20% were probably more reasonable, because he was uncertain that the CMI pads in larger sizes would perform as well.

Industry Practice

Industry sources indicated that as many as 75% of pile-driving contractors owned their hammers, and most owned at least one crane and set of leads. To determine the contractors' cost of doing business, CMI studied expenses of small contractors who rented equipment for pile-driving jobs. These numbers were readily available and avoided the problem of allocating the cost of a purchased crane or hammer to a particular job.

Standard industry practice for equipment rental used a three-week month and a three-day workweek.[5] There was no explanation for this, other than tradition, but most equipment renters set their rates this way. The cost of renting the necessary equipment and the labor cost for a job similar to that performed by Colerick were estimated as shown in **Table A**.

Table A　Equipment Rental, Labor, and Overhead Costs

| | | Per Standard | | | |
		Month	Week	Per Hour	Average Cost per Real Hour[a]
1.	Diesel hammer	$4,500–7,200	$1,500–2,400	$62.50–100.00	$34
2.	Crane	8,000–10,000	2,667–3,334	111.00–140.00	52
3.	Leads @ $20 per foot per month (assume 70 feet)	1,400	467	19.44	8
4.	Labor[b]—3 laborers @ $6–8 per hour each			18.00–24.00	21
	1 crane operator			8.00–12.00	10
	1 foreman			12.00–14.00	13
5.	Overhead[c] (office, trucks, oil/gas, tools, etc.)			100.00	100

(Casewriter's note: Please use average cost per real hour in all calculations, for uniformity in class discussion.)

[a]These costs were calculated from a rounded midpoint of the estimates. Hammer, crane, and lead costs were obtained by dividing standard monthly costs by 4.33 weeks per month and 40 hours per week.

[b]Labor was paid on a 40–hour week, and a 4.33-week month. One-shift operation (40 hours per week) was standard in the industry.

[c]Most contractors calculated overhead on the basis of "working" hours, not standard hours.

_____

[5] This means that a contractor who rented equipment for one calendar month was charged only the "three-week" price, but had the equipment for the whole calendar month. The same was true of the "three-day week." Contractors generally tried to use the equipment for as much time per week or per month as possible. Thus they rented it on a "three-week" month but used it on a "4.33-week" month.

Hidden costs also played an important role. For every hour actually spent driving piles, a contractor could spend 20 to 40 minutes moving the crane into position. Another 10% to 15% was added to cover scheduling delays, mistakes, and other unavoidable problems. Thus, the real cost per hour was usually substantially more than the initial figures showed. Reducing the driving time or pad changing time did not usually affect the time lost on delays and moving.

All these figures were based on a job that utilized 55-foot piles and 11 $\frac{1}{2}$-inch pads. Although this was a common size, much larger jobs requiring substantially bigger material were frequent. A stack of 11 $\frac{1}{2}$-inch asbestos pads weighed between 30 and 40 pounds; the 30-inch size could weigh seven to eight times more. Each 11 $\frac{1}{2}$-inch CMI pad weighed 15 $\frac{1}{2}$ pounds. The bigger sizes, being much more difficult to handle, could contribute significantly to unproductive time on a job. (See **Exhibit 5**.)

Most contracts were awarded on a revenue-per-foot basis. Thus, contractors bid by estimating the amount of time it would take to drive the specified piles the distance required by the architectural engineers. After totaling costs and adding a percentage for profit, they submitted figures broken down into dollars per foot. The cost depended on the size of the piles and the type of soil to be penetrated. The $5 per foot that Colerick charged was not atypical, but prices could be considerably greater.

Test Results

The management of CMI was extremely pleased by how well its cushion pads had performed. Not only had they lasted the entire job, eliminating the downtime required for changeover, but other advantages had become apparent. For example, after 500 feet of driving, the average temperature for the asbestos pads was between 600°F and 700°F, which created great difficulty when they had to be replaced. The crew handling them was endangered, and substantial time was wasted waiting for them to cool. (This accounted for a major portion of the time lost to changeovers.)

The CMI pads, in contrast, never went above 250°F and could be handled almost immediately with protective gloves. This indicated that substantial energy lost in heat by the asbestos pads was being used more efficiently to drive the piles with CMI pads. In addition, the outstanding resiliency of the CMI product seemed to account for a 33% faster driving time, which translated into significant savings.

In talking with construction site personnel, CMI researchers also found that most were becoming wary of the asbestos pads' well-publicized health dangers. Many had expressed a desire to use some other material and were pleased that the new pads contained no asbestos.

The CMI management was quite happy with these results; Colerick was ecstatic. Understandably, Colerick became quite anxious to buy more pads and began pressing Tom Simpson to quote prices.

A Second Test

To confirm the results from the Colerick test, CMI asked Fazio Construction to try the pads on a job in New Brighton, Pennsylvania. This job required 300 45-foot concrete piles to be driven 40 feet into the ground. Asbestos pads (11 $\frac{1}{2}$ inches) were again used for comparison. Total job revenue was $108,000, or $9 per foot, and Fazio would have paid $40 for each set of 12 asbestos pads used. The results from this test are shown as follows:

Cumberland Metal Industries: Engineered Products Division, 1980

		Asbestos	CMI
1.	Feet driven per hour while pile driver was at work (does not consider downtime)	160	200
2.	Piles driven per set of pads	6	300
3.	Number of pads per set	12	5
4.	Number of sets required	50	1
5.	Number of set changes	50	1
6.	Time required for change per set	20 mins.	4 mins.
7.	Fazio cost per set	$40	Not charged

The Market

Projected Size

There were virtually no statistics from which a potential U.S. market for cushion pads could be determined, so Simpson had to make several assumptions based on the information he could gather. A 1977 report by *Construction Engineering* magazine estimated that approximately 13,000 pile hammers were owned by companies directly involved in pile driving. Industry sources estimated that another 6,500 to 13,000 were leased. He assumed that this total of 19,500 to 26,000 hammers would operate about 25 weeks per year (because of seasonality) and that they would be used 30 hours per week (because of moving time, repairs, scheduling problems, and other factors).

Simpson further assumed that an average actual driving figure (including time to change pads and so on) for most jobs was 20 feet per hour, which amounted to between 290 million and 390 million feet of piles driven annually. To be conservative, he also assumed that a set of curled metal pads (four initially installed, plus two added after the originals lost some resiliency) would drive 10,000 feet.

Purchase Influences

In the pile-driving business, as in other parts of the construction industry, a number of entities participated in purchases. The CMI management was able to identify six types of influences.

1. *Pile hammer manufacturers.* A number of manufacturers sold hammers in the United States although many were imported from Western Europe and Japan. The leading domestic producer in 1979 was Vulcan Iron Works of New Orleans, whose Model #1 had become the standard used by architectural engineers specifying equipment for a job. Simpson did not feel these manufacturers would purchase a large dollar volume of cushion pads, but they could be very influential in recommendations.

2. *Architectural/Consulting engineers.* Pile driving required significant expertise in determining the needs of a construction project. Thorough stress analysis and other mathematical analysis were necessary. Because of the risks in building the expensive projects usually supported by piles, the industry looked to architectural/consulting engineers as the ultimate authorities on all aspects of the business. Consequently, these firms were very detailed in specifying the materials and techniques to be used on a project. They always specified hammers and

frequently mentioned pads. The CMI management felt that, although no sales would come from these people, they could be one of the most important purchase influences.

3. *Soil consultants.* These consultants were similar to the architectural/consulting engineers, but were consulted only on extraordinary conditions.

4. *Pile hammer distributing/renting companies.* This group was an important influence because it provided pads to the contractors. In fact, renting companies often included the first set of pads free. CMI management felt that these companies would handle the cushion pads they could most easily sell and might even hesitate to provide pads that enabled a contractor to return equipment faster.

5. *Engineering/Construction contractors.* The contracting portion of the industry was divided among large international firms and smaller independents. The former almost always participated in the bigger, more sophisticated jobs. Companies like Conmaco and Raymond International not only contracted to drive piles, but also designed jobs, specified material, and even manufactured their own equipment. It was clear to Simpson that if he was to succeed in getting CMI pads used on bigger, complex construction projects, CMI would have to solicit this group actively on a very sophisticated level.

6. *Independent pile-driving contractors.* These contractors represented the "frontline buying influence." Their primary objective was to make money. They were very knowledgeable about the practical aspects of pile driving, but not very sophisticated.

No national industry associations influenced this business, but some regional organizations played a minor part. Contractors and others talked freely, although few were willing to reveal competitive secrets. The company was unsure how important word-of-mouth communication would be. Very little was published about the pile-driving industry, although construction-oriented magazines like *Louisiana Contractor* occasionally reported on pile-driving contractors and their jobs. These magazines featured advertising by suppliers to the trade, mostly equipment dealers and supply houses. One industry supplier, Associated Pile and Fitting Corporation, sponsored professional-level "Piletalk" seminars in various cities, bringing designers, contractors, and equipment developers together "to discuss practical aspects of installation of driven piles."

Another potential influence was Professor R. Stephen McCormack of Pennsylvania A&M University. He had established a department to study pile driving and had become a respected authority on its theoretical aspects. Sophisticated engineering/construction firms and many architectural consultants were familiar with his work and helped support it. Cumberland management felt that his endorsement of the operational performance of CMI cushion pads would greatly enhance industry acceptance. The company submitted the pads for testing by Dr. McCormack in the fall of 1979, and although the final results were not yet available he had expressed considerable enthusiasm. Final results were expected by early 1980.

Competitive Products and Channels of Distribution

The pile-driving industry had paid very little attention to cushion pads before CMI's involvement. Everyone used them and took them for granted, but no one attempted to promote pads. No manufacturers dominated the business. In fact, most pads came unbranded, having been cut from larger pieces of asbestos or micarta by small, anonymous job shops.

Distribution of pads was also ambiguous. Hammer sales and rental outlets provided them, heavy construction supply houses carried them, pile manufacturers sometimes offered them, and a miscellaneous assortment of other outlets occasionally sold them as a service.[6] The smaller pads sold for $2 to $3 each; larger ones sold for between $5 and $10. Three dollars each was typical for 11 1/2 inch pads. The profit margin for a distributor was usually adequate—in the area of 30% to 40%—but the dollar profit did not compare well with that of other equipment lines. Most outlets carried pads as a necessary part of the business, but none featured them as a work-saving tool.

The CMI management felt it could be totally flexible in establishing an organization to approach the market. It toyed with the idea of a direct sales force and its own distribution outlets, but eventually began to settle on signing construction-oriented manufacturers' representatives,[7] who would sell to a variety of distributors and supply houses. The company feared an uphill struggle to convince the sales and distribution channels that there really was a market for the new pad. Management expected considerable difficulty in finding outlets willing to devote the attention necessary for success, but it also felt that once the initial barriers had been penetrated, most of the marketplace would be anxious to handle the product.

The Pricing Decision

Simpson had projected cost data developed by his manufacturing engineers. **Exhibit 6** shows two sets of numbers: one utilized existing equipment; the other reflected the purchase of $50,000 of permanent tooling. In both cases, the estimated volume was 250 cushion pads per month. Additional equipment could be added at a cost of $75,000 per 250 pads per month of capacity, including permanent tooling like that which could be purchased for $50,000.

Both sets of numbers were based on the assumption that only one pad size would be manufactured; in other words, the numbers in the 11 1/2 -inch size were based on manufacturing only this size for a year. This was done because CMI had no idea of the potential sales mix among product sizes. Management knew that 11 1/2 inches was the most popular size, but the information available on popularity of the other sizes was vague. CMI accounting personnel believed these numbers would not vary dramatically with a mix of sizes.

Corporate management usually burdened CMI products with a charge equal to 360% of direct labor to cover the overhead of its large engineering staff. Simpson was uncertain how this would apply to the new product, because little engineering had been done and excess capacity was to be used initially for manufacturing. Although it was allocated on a variable basis, he thought he might consider the overhead "fixed" for his analysis. Corporate management expected a contribution margin after all manufacturing costs of 40% to 50% of selling price.

Simpson was enthusiastic about the potential success of this new product. The Engineered Products Division was particularly pleased to offer something with such high dollar potential, especially since in the past, a "large customer" of the division had purchased only about $10,000 per year.

---

[6] Supply houses were "hardware stores" for contractors and carried a general line of products, including lubricants, work gloves, and maintenance supplies. Distributors, in contrast, tended to be more equipment oriented and to sell a narrower line of merchandise.

[7] Manufacturers' representatives were agents (sometimes single people, sometimes organizations) who sold non-competing products for commission. They typically did *not* take title to the merchandise and did *not* extend credit.

He was still uncertain how to market the pads and how to reach the various purchase influences. Advertising and promotion also concerned him because there were no precedents for this product or market.

For the moment, however, Simpson's primary consideration was pricing. He had promised to call Colerick Foundation Company by the end of the week, and Minicucci was anxious to review his decision with him. He hoped other prospects would be calling as soon as word about the pads' test performance got around.

Exhibit 1   Engineered Products Division Organization Chart

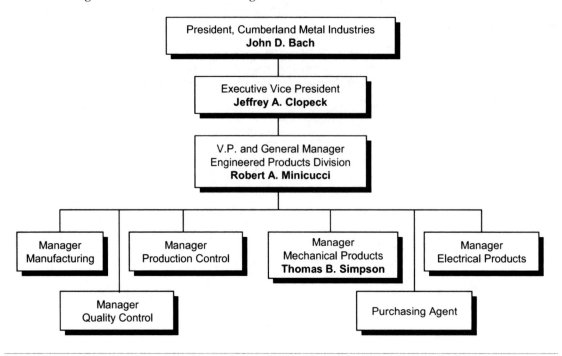

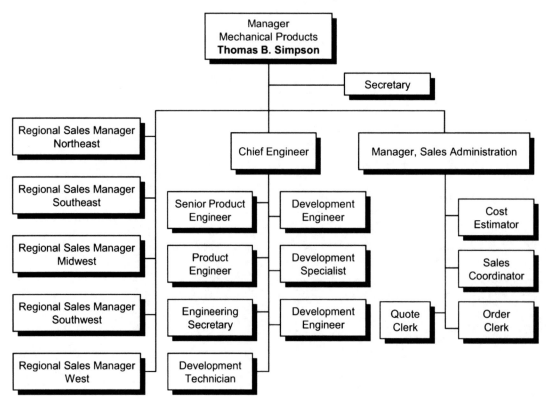

Exhibit 2   Income Statement

December 31	1979	1978
Net sales	$18,524,428	$20,465,057
Costs and expenses		
Cost of sales	11,254,927	11,759,681
Selling expenses	2,976,396	2,711,320
General and administrative expenses	2,204,291	2,362,528
	16,435,614	16,833,529
Income from operations	2,088,814	3,631,528
Other income (expense)		
Dividend income	208,952	—
Interest income	72,966	186,611
Interest expense	(40,636)	(31,376)
	241,282	155,235
Income before income taxes	2,330,096	3,786,763
Provision for income taxes	1,168,830	1,893,282
Net income	1,161,266	1,893,481
Net income per share	$1.39	$2.16

Exhibit 3   Typical Steam- or Air-Operated Pile Driver with Helmet and Cushion Pad

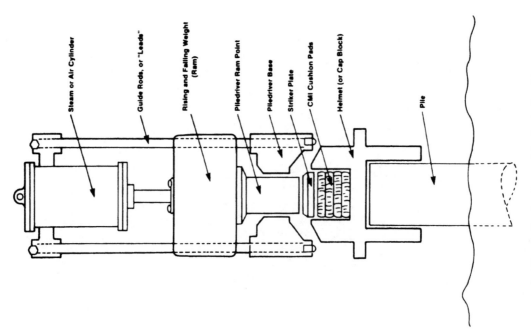

Pile hammer inside leads driving a steel H-beam into the ground

Steam or Air Cylinder

Guide Rods, or "Leads"

Rising and Falling Weight
(Ram)

Piledriver Ram Point

Piledriver Base

Striker Plate

CMI Cushion Pads

Helmet (or Cap Block)

Pile

A schematic diagram of typical pile driver

Exhibit 3 (continued)

CMI pile-driving pad in position in helmet

Close-up of hammer driving pile (most of the pile is already in the ground)

Exhibit 4   Close-up of CMI Curled Metal Cushion Pad for Pile Driving

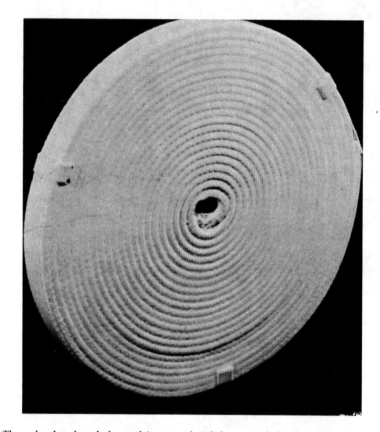

The calendered curled metal is wound tightly around the central point of a flat metallic disk. (The disk is on the back side of the pad from this view.) Soldered tabs secure the curled metal to the disk. The entire structure is coated with polyvinyl-chloride.

Exhibit 5   Curled Metal Cushion Pad Standard Sizes

Diameter (inches)	Thickness (inches)	Weight (pounds)
11 1/2	1	15 1/2
14	1	23
17 1/2	1	36
19 3/4	1	48
23	1	64
30	1	110

Cumberland Metal Industries: Engineered Products Division, 1980

Exhibit 6   Two Sets of Projected Manufacturing Costs

	Size					
	11 ½"	14"	17 ½"	19 ¾"	23"	30"
Estimates per Pad with Existing Equipment						
Variable						
Material	$15.64	$20.57	$31.81	$40.39	$53.16	$95.69
Labor	28.80	33.07	50.02	57.07	69.16	118.36
Total variable	44.44	53.64	81.83	97.46	122.32	214.05
Fixed factory overhead						
@ 360% direct labor	103.68	119.05	180.07	205.45	248.98	426.10
Total manufacturing cost	$148.12	$172.69	$261.90	$302.91	$371.30	$640.15
Estimated with Purchase of $50,000 of Permanent Tooling						
Variable						
Material	$15.64	$20.57	$31.81	$40.39	$53.16	$95.69
Labor	11.64	15.25	21.85	26.95	30.57	56.09
Total variable	27.28	35.82	53.66	67.34	83.73	151.78
Fixed factory overhead						
@ 360% direct labor	41.90	54.90	78.66	97.02	110.05	201.92
Total manufacturing cost	$69.18	$90.72	$132.32	$164.36	$193.78	$353.70

Note: Estimated volume was 250 cushion pads per month.

HARVARD | BUSINESS | SCHOOL

9-502-030

REV: JULY 10, 2006

YOUNGME MOON

Aqualisa Quartz: Simply a Better Shower

Plumbing hasn't changed since Roman times.

—Tim Pestell, Aqualisa national sales manager

Harry Rawlinson (HBS '90) shrugged out of his overcoat and headed to the reception desk of the South Kent County Marriott. "Can you direct me to the breakfast room?" he asked, "I'm meeting some guests from America." The receptionist pointed toward a hallway lined with photographs of the region's golf fairways and putting greens. "It's just to the left down there," she said. As he strode down the narrow corridor, Rawlinson, managing director of Aqualisa (see **Exhibit 1**), a U.K. shower manufacturer, felt a surge of energy. He had been looking forward to this opportunity to discuss an HBS case possibility.

In May 2001 Aqualisa had launched the Quartz shower, the first significant product innovation in the U.K. shower market since—well, to Rawlinson's mind—since *forever*. But here it was early September 2001, and the euphoria surrounding the product's initial launch had long since faded. Rawlinson knew the Quartz was technologically leaps and bounds above other U.K. showers in terms of water pressure, ease of installation, use, and design. But for some reason, it simply wasn't selling.

The U.K. Shower Market

Rawlinson leaned forward as he began to explain his situation. Showers in the U.K. were plagued with problems. While everyone had a bathtub, only about 60% of U.K. homes had showers. Archaic plumbing, some of it dating to the Victorian era, was still common in many homes. For the most part this plumbing was gravity fed; a cold-water tank or cistern sat somewhere in the roof, while a separate boiler and cylinder were needed to store hot water in a nearby airing cupboard.

Gravity-fed plumbing meant poor-to-low water pressure, about 3 to 4 liters per minute.[1] Gravity-fed plumbing also created frequent fluctuations in pressure, which caused the temperature to noticeably vary from minute to minute. If the pressure from the cold-water pipe decreased momentarily, the flow from the hot water pipe would increase, immediately raising the temperature.

---

[1] Water pressure in the United States, in contrast, is generally at least 18 liters per minute.

Professor Youngme Moon and Research Associate Kerry Herman prepared this case. HBS cases are developed solely as the basis for class discussion. Cases are not intended to serve as endorsements, sources of primary data, or illustrations of effective or ineffective management. Some data have been modified or disguised.

These two problems—low pressure and fluctuations in temperature—were typically addressed through the use of either electric showers or special U.K. shower valves.

1. **Electric showers** used water from the cold water supply. Electrical heating elements in the shower instantaneously heated the water to the required temperature, eliminating the need for a boiler to store hot water. While this made electric showers convenient for small bathrooms, the electrical components were usually mounted in a bulky white box that was visible in the shower stall. In addition, electric showers did nothing to address the poor water flow of many showers in U.K. homes, since the flow was limited by the amount of energy that could be applied to heat the water instantaneously. Aqualisa sold electric showers mostly under a separate brand name, the "Gainsborough" brand. (See **Exhibit 2** for shower sales by type and brand.)

2. **Mixer shower valves** came in two types: manual and thermostatic. Both types blended hot and cold water to create a comfortable temperature, but while thermostatic valves controlled the temperature automatically, manual valves required the user to manually find the right temperature mix. Installing a mixer valve meant excavating the bathroom wall, which was often a two-day job. If a user wanted to boost water pressure, an additional booster pump (typically costing from €350 to €600) could be installed to enhance the flow rate.

   The Aquavalve 609 was the company's core product in the mixer-shower-valve category. At about 60,000 units per year, it was by far Aqualisa's top-selling shower. It was regarded by plumbers as being a high-quality, reliable mixer shower with state-of-the-art technology. It cost about €155 to manufacture and sold (at retail) for €675 to €750. The Aquavalve 609 was thermostatic and could be supplemented by an Aquaforce booster pump to create stronger pressure.

3. **Integral power showers** consisted of a single compact unit that combined a thermostatic mixer valve and a booster pump. Although they provided up to 18 liters of blended water per minute, they had to be mounted in the shower, resulting in the presence of a bulky box on the wall. In addition, these units were generally regarded as being less reliable than a mixer-shower and booster-pump combination. The Aquastream Thermostatic was Aqualisa's primary product in this category. It cost about €175 to produce and sold (at retail) for about €670. At about 20,000 units per year, it was Aqualisa's strongest-selling shower in the power shower category.

Most consumers could readily identify what they disliked about their showers—poor pressure and varying temperature being at the top of the list. But there were other complaints as well. Showers often broke down, or "went wrong," as Rawlinson described. "They break after awhile. The mechanisms get gummed up with lime scale, making the valves stiff and hard to turn; the seals start to leak, or they go out of date." As a result, consumers complained about hard-to-turn valves, leaky seals, and worn-out showers. (Almost half the U.K. shower market consisted of sales of replacement showers—see **Exhibit 3**.) On the other hand, consumers were generally uninformed about showers, and there was little understanding of product options (see **Exhibit 4**). Brand awareness was low; only one company in the market (Triton) had managed to build brand awareness at the consumer level.

Shower buyers in the U.K. tended to fall into one of three pricing segments: premium, standard, and value. Consumers in the premium segment typically shopped in showrooms; they took for granted high performance and service, and for them style determined their selection. Consumers in the standard price range tended to emphasize performance and service; they usually relied on an independent plumber to recommend or select a product for them. Consumers in the value segment

Aqualisa Quartz: Simply a Better Shower   502-030

were primarily concerned with convenience and price; they liked to avoid solutions that required any excavation and tended to rely on an independent plumber to select a product. (See **Figure A** for Aqualisa's core product offerings in the various shower categories.)

Figure A   Aqualisa's Core Product Offerings in the Various Shower Categories[2]

| Type of Shower | | Aqualisa's Core Product Offerings | | |
		Value	Standard	Premium
Electric Shower	• Does not require hot water supply • Results in bulky box on the wall • Low flow rate	Gainsborough Retail: €95	Gainsborough Retail: €155	Aquastyle Retail: €230
Mixer Shower	• Requires both hot and cold water supply • Requires additional pump to address pressure problems • Installation typically requires excavation of bathroom	Aquavalve Retail: €390	Aquavalve 609 Retail: €715	
Power Shower	• Requires both hot and cold water supply • Results in bulky box on the wall • Regarded as less reliable than a mixer-shower and pump combination	Aquastream Manual Retail: €480	Aquastream Thermostatic Retail: €670	

Source: Aqualisa.

In addition, there was a sizeable do-it-yourself (DIY) market in the U.K. Do-it-yourselfers generally shopped at large retail outlets that catered to them (for example, the popular B&Q, which modeled itself after Home Depot in the United States). These customers were primarily interested in inexpensive models that were easy to install, even though the DIY products were bulky and unattractive. Electric showers were the overwhelming choice in this segment. They could be adapted to all water systems and could be installed in a day; they were particularly popular among landlords and apartment dwellers.

Finally, there was a significant property developer market in the U.K. Most developers did not need to worry about pressure problems because new homes were almost exclusively built with high-pressure systems. Developers faced a different set of issues, preferring reliable, nice-looking products that could work in multiple settings. Developers were also price-sensitive; with the exception of luxury builders, most developers did not feel the need to invest in premium valves. Developers usually had relationships with independent plumbers who installed whatever product they selected.

Aqualisa sold to developers under its ShowerMax brand, which was available only through specialist contract outlets. Elements of the Aquavalve technology had been redesigned and re-branded for the ShowerMax product line and optimized for developers' specific needs. Because new homes did not use gravity systems, ShowerMax could deliver a high-pressure shower—with

---

[2] Aqualisa offered a variety of other specialty shower models in each of these categories. The differences between these showers were primarily stylistic (e.g., contemporary, antique, brass, etc.).

Aquavalve technology—at a significantly lower cost. Rawlinson commented, "Aqualisa's core products are too expensive for them because of extra features aimed at the retail market. Even at a discounted price, they consider Aqualisa too high-end. But a cut-down product branded "ShowerMax" just for them, at the right price—they love it."

Rawlinson continued:

> Real breakthroughs are pretty rare in the shower market. Innovations are primarily cosmetic. Most of the major manufacturers recycle their product line and relaunch their main products about every four or five years. It refreshes your brand, but market share doesn't really change. At Aqualisa, we've tended to do a relaunch every three to four years. Aesthetically we've changed the look, and we've made incremental technological improvements to boost the performance and quality, but it's basically been the same mechanisms inside. These aren't breakthrough innovations we're talking about.

Channels of Distribution

Showers in the U.K. were sold through a variety of channels (see **Exhibits 5** and **6**), including trade shops, distributors, showrooms, and DIY outlets.

Trade shops. Trade shops (or plumbers' merchants) carried products across all available brands. Their primary customer was the plumber, who worked for developers, showrooms, contractors, or directly for consumers. Trade merchants tended to stock whatever there was demand for. The Aqualisa brand was available in 40% of trade shops. As Rawlinson put it: "The staff in these outlets don't have the time to learn all the features and benefits of the 45,000 items they offer. They focus on making sure they have the right stock of products that are in demand. Their customers are looking for reliable product availability more than technical advice."

Showrooms. Distributors supplied showrooms, which tended to be more high-end. Showroom "consultants" typically led consumers through the process of selecting and designing a bathroom "solution." A shower might be one small part of an overall renovation project. Various shower and bath options were displayed in the showroom, and although no inventory was held on location, these ensembles allowed the consumer a chance to view the product in a pleasant environment. Showrooms preferred to carry high-end product lines and brands (for example, Hansgrohe, a high-end German brand) unavailable in other channels. Showrooms also offered installation services by subcontracting with contractors and independent plumbers. There were about 2,000 showrooms in the U.K.; the Aqualisa brand was sold in about 25% of them.

DIY Sheds. Do-it-yourself retail outlets like B&Q offered discount, mass-market, do-it-yourself products. Electric showers, because they were cheaper and easier to retrofit, led sales in this channel. The Aqualisa brand was unavailable through this channel, but its Gainsborough brand was available in 70% of the approximately 3,000 DIY outlets in the U.K.

Plumbers (Installers)

There were about 10,000 master plumbers in the U.K. Plumbers had to undergo several years of training and three years of apprenticeship to become master plumbers. There was a significant shortage of master plumbers in the U.K., and as a result, consumers often had to wait six months before a plumber could take on a new job.

A standard shower installation was usually a two-day job and required significant bathroom excavation.[3] Plumbers—who installed 40 to 50 showers a year—charged about €40 to €80 per hour, plus the cost of excavation and materials (plumbers usually passed the cost of the shower and other materials on to the consumer with a small markup).   Because prices to consumers were usually quotes as lump sums, consumers were often unaware of how the costs broke down (labor, materials, excavation, and so on).

For plumbers, unfamiliar products could present unknown performance problems, and a bungled installation often required a second visit, paid for out of the plumber's pocket. For this reason, plumbers generally preferred to install a single shower brand and were extremely reluctant to switch brands. Loyalty to a single brand created expertise in a given brand's installation idiosyncrasies and failure problems. Over time, plumbers also liked to familiarize themselves with the service they could expect from a manufacturer.

As a general rule, plumbers distrusted innovation. For example, in the 1980s some manufacturers had introduced electronic "push-button" controls for temperature settings. Rawlinson recalled: "The mechanisms were poorly designed and didn't work well at all. Ever since that, there's been a great deal of skepticism toward anything that seems technologically newfangled—especially if it involves electronics."

The Development of the Quartz Shower Valve

Historically, Aqualisa's reputation had always been strong in the U.K. shower market; the company was generally recognized as having top quality showers, a premium brand, and great service. Aqualisa's market share ranked it number two in mixing valves and number three in the overall U.K. shower market. (See **Exhibit 7** for additional information on Aqualisa's financials.)

However, when Rawlinson joined the company in 1998, he believed it was vulnerable, for several reasons. First, Rawlinson believed that other companies were catching up to Aqualisa in terms of product quality. Second, Rawlinson feared that the market was beginning to perceive Aqualisa products as being overpriced (see **Exhibit 8**). Third, while Aqualisa's service was still regarded as being "great," actual service had slipped over the past few years. And finally, about 10% of Aqualisa showers still "went wrong," a percentage that hadn't improved in many years.   Rawlinson remembered:

When I first joined Aqualisa in May of 1998, what I found was a highly profitable company that was quite comfortable with its niche in the market. It had 25% net return on sales and was enjoying 5% to 10% growth in a mature market. Everyone was happy. But I was worried. I knew the current points of difference were eroding and that eventually the market might implode on us. From the start, I firmly believed that the future was to focus on innovation.

Rawlinson's first priority was to build a research and development (R&D) team:

We brought together a top-notch team of outsiders and insiders to look at the future of showers. We had engineers, R&D, our sales and marketing director, and a market research guy. We did research studies to understand peoples' problems and attitudes to showering. We had a top industrial designer and a bunch of Cambridge scientists who apply technology to industrial applications. We put all these people into a huddle—held brainstorming sessions,

---

[3] Typically, the plumber would either excavate himself, or he would subcontract the work to a plasterer. The price plumbers charged for excavation varied significantly.

with flip charts and felt-tip pens. And we came up with all kinds of things to improve in a shower.

As a result of their market research, Rawlinson realized that the consumer wanted a shower that looked great, delivered good pressure at stable temperatures, was easy to use, and didn't break down. Plumbers wanted a shower that was easy to install, with a guarantee to not break down or require servicing. The team's brainstorming led to some real breakthroughs. Rawlinson noted:

> The breakthrough idea was to locate the mechanism that mixes the water remotely—*away* from the shower. All the problems with showers come down to the fact that you have to put a clumsy, mechanical control right where the user doesn't want it—*in* the shower. And that's why you get these big bulky boxes on the shower wall. Or you're constrained to put the mechanism somewhere in the wall behind the shower—equally difficult and costly to install or repair. But locating the mechanism remotely—all of a sudden that opened up all kinds of opportunities because now you didn't necessarily have to excavate.

> The problem was, how could a user control a mechanism that was located remotely? And that's when we brought the electronics people in. Of course, that generated a lot of skepticism, because electronics had flopped so terribly in the '80s. But nobody had ever thought of using the electronics to control the valve remotely. And when we came up with the idea, we realized very quickly that it had *huge* potential.

Once the product started to take shape, field tests were next. Rawlinson arranged for about 60 consumer field test sites, installing showers in the homes of sales reps, company personnel, and friends of friends. Feedback from the field tests prompted constant modifications. He recalled:

> Consumers told us they wanted maximum pressure. But once we gave them maximum pressure (about 18 liters per minute) consumers felt it was wasteful. So we had to give them the option to run at two-thirds speed—which they liked more than maximum pressure.

> With the temperature settings, it was the same thing. We knew from our research that the optimal water temperature was 41° [Celsius]; anything above that would be uncomfortably hot. So we created this temperature control that had an upper limit of 41°. But people hated the fact that it required them to turn the valve all the way to the right, into the "red zone" on the indicator. Even though nobody wanted their water hotter than 41°, they all wanted the *option* of being able to make the temperature hotter. So we reset the maximum to 45°, people set their temperature at 41°, and everyone liked that much better.

After three years of development—during which the company spent €5.8 million—the result was a radically different kind of shower (called Quartz) that cost the company about €175 to €230 to make. By this time, the company had invested in a new state-of-the-art testing facility, had acquired nine patents, and had grown its engineering team from 6 to 20. Several additional products were in advanced stages of development, while dozens of other ideas were in the early stages of the new-product development pipeline.

The Quartz: A Breakthrough in Shower Technology

The Quartz came in two versions. The Quartz Standard Shower was designed for installations that already had, or did not need, a pump; the Quartz Pumped Shower included a pump.

To install the Quartz shower, the plumber had to identify a physical space to accommodate the remote processor, which was about the size of a shoe box. The processor contained the thermostatic mixing valve, and when applicable, the pump. The location of the processor could be anywhere within reasonable proximity to the shower—under a cabinet, behind a wall, inside a closet, in the ceiling, wherever. The device could be mounted horizontally, vertically, or on its side, depending on space constraints. The only requirements were that it had to be in a location where cold and hot water could be piped into the processor, and it had to be plugged into a standard power outlet. Once these requirements were met and the processor was in place, a single pipe fed the mixed water from the processor to the showerhead. Because of the flexibility associated with locating the processor remotely, excavation of the bathroom could often be avoided altogether. Instead, a plumber had only to drill a single hole (to accommodate the pipe feeding the mixed water to the showerhead, along with a data cable) into the ceiling above the shower (see **Figure B**).[4]

Figure B   The Quartz Technology

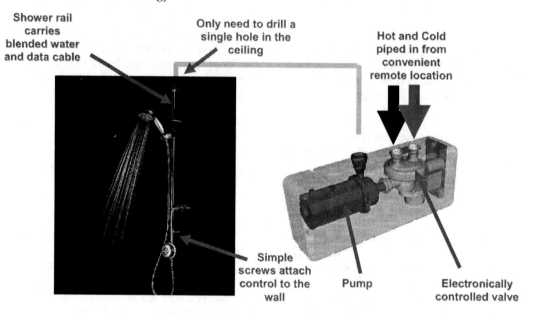

Source: Aqualisa.

The benefits of Quartz were significant. Whereas a traditional shower installation took two days, some plumbers were already reporting an installation time of a half-day for the Quartz. Plumbers were finding that the installation was so straightforward that they could even send their young apprentices—many with little or no experience—to complete the entire job. Rawlinson had spoken to several plumbers during the field trials, "They raved about it. They said, 'It's just what we want! We need something like this that we can push-fit-connect-you're done. It's not in the wall, and it's very easy to use.'"

---

[4] The ease of installation was a big selling point for the Quartz. In fact, it was so easy that the installation guide itself was being used in Quartz's promotional and sales materials.

For the consumer, the Quartz shower provided efficient and reliable water pressure and temperature. In addition, it featured a "one-touch" control mounted on the shower wall. The easy-to-use push-button control light on the valve flashed red until the desired temperature was reached (see **Figure C**). Rawlinson remembered that this had been another feature with unexpected psychological benefits:

> When consumers turn a traditional shower on, they almost always turn the shower to very hot … and then wait for it to warm up. They usually have to stick their hand in the shower a few times until they feel it's hot enough to get in. Once they're in the shower, they immediately start fiddling with the controls again. It's incredibly inefficient and inconvenient.

> With our Quartz technology, the temperature control is automatic—there's no more fiddling. You don't have to manipulate anything anymore. Just set the temperature once, and leave it on that setting. When you want to use the shower, just press a button, and you've turned the shower on. When the red light stops flashing, you know the water's at the right temperature. Get in.

During field trials, consumers loved it. "We call it the 'wow' factor," Rawlinson said. "They loved how it looked; it delivered great power, and now it had neat fittings and push-button controls that lit up. Parents loved it because it was safe for their kids to use on their own. The elderly loved it because they didn't have to fight with stiff valves. What wasn't to love?"

Figure C   The Quartz Thermostatic Control

Source: Aqualisa.

Rawlinson was already anticipating upcoming product releases. In a few months, Aqualisa would be ready to launch a Body Jet product that fit easily on top of the Quartz control valve, creating several jets of water that sprayed horizontally from the wall onto one's body. This feature was popular in spas and health clubs; women particularly liked it because it allowed them to shower without getting their hair wet. The R&D team had also just finished designing a "slave" remote for the Quartz. Rawlinson described it: "Imagine waking up in the morning, rolling over, and pushing a 'remote control' next to your bed that turns your shower on. By the time you stumble in the bathroom, your shower is ready with the water at the right temperature, waiting for you to get in. Because we're dealing with electronics, the wireless technology to do this is almost trivial."

In fact, Rawlinson and the R&D team could spend endless hours coming up with new product ideas; as Rawlinson liked to say, "Once you put a computer in the bathroom, the potential is unlimited!"

To launch the new product, Aqualisa had hit the major shows, like the Bathroom Expo in London in May 2001. At the Expo, the Quartz had been awarded the top prize.[5] Press events had been coordinated with demonstrations. The trade press had raved about the "cleverness" of the product and its "elegant design." One reporter wrote:

> Imagine a shower that takes less than a day to fit, doesn't have flow problems, offers accurate temperature control, is simplicity itself to use and comes in versions to suit all water systems. It sounds too good to be true—but after three years of brainstorming . . . Aqualisa has achieved the apparently impossible with a product that takes a genuinely new look at a set of old problems—and solves them.[6]

Other reviewers had been similarly positive, and the Quartz had been featured on the covers of several prominent trade journals.

Initial Sales Results

Aqualisa had a 20-person sales force that sold to distributors, trade shops, showrooms, developers, and plumbers. Tim Pestell, Aqualisa's national sales manager, described the sales team's priorities: "Our sales force spends about 90% of their time on maintaining existing accounts— servicing existing customers: distributors, trade shops, contractors, showrooms, and developers. Ten percent of their time is spent on developing new customers." Aqualisa's sales force also had long-standing direct relationships with a group of plumbers—"our plumbers" as director of marketing Martyn Denny called them—who were very loyal to the Aqualisa brand.

With the launch of the Quartz, the Aqualisa sales force had contacted its network of plumbers, calling face-to-face to introduce and explain the new product, but few actual sales had resulted. Indeed, despite all the early excitement over the product, and despite being made available in all of Aqualisa's normal channels, very few units had sold in the first four months on the market. Rawlinson worried:

> Our channel partners are sitting there having bought a thousand of these Quartz products, and they've sold 81. The poor product manager is looking pretty stupid at this stage. This is a huge problem for us—pretty soon they're going to write this off as a failure and forget about us. I can see a scenario in six months' time where real sales in the market—currently about 15 units a day—are still down at 30 or 40 units a day. We'll look like a niche product. We've got to sell 100 or 200 a day to break through to the mainstream.

Part of the problem was that plumbers were wary of innovation, particularly any innovation involving electronics. Rawlinson told the story of a personal friend who had to insist that her plumber install a Quartz:

> His initial reaction was negative. He said, "Oh no, I wouldn't put one of these in, Madam. I've had these electronic showers before. They don't work." She insisted and made him put it

---

[5] "Showered with Success," *Bathroom Journal*, June 2001, p. 13.

[6] Ibid.

in. He told her it would take two days. He was done by lunchtime the first day. And he said, "That was so easy. Can I have the brochure?" And now he's got two or three more jobs. So once a plumber puts one in, he's a convert.

Pestell, however, noted that given the conservative nature of most plumbers, "Adoption is a long, slow process. It takes time." In addition, he pointed out:

> Some people at the company think the Quartz will eventually replace our core product— the Aquavalve—and become mainstream. I think it's really a niche product—it's good for homes with children, or for the elderly and the handicapped. It's easy to use, safe and so on, but we can't forget our core products every time we launch something new. The Aquavalve is our bread and butter, and it can go away if no one's watching.

Denny concurred, "How do we pitch our other products alongside Quartz? Right now, if Quartz is mentioned, our salesmen tend to gloss over our other products. In fact, to sell the Quartz, they have to point out *deficiencies* in our existing products. That doesn't really make any sense, does it?"

According to Rawlinson, the only place Quartz seemed to be gaining any traction was in the showrooms:

> Showrooms are traditionally quite a niche market. But I think we've made some penetration into that sector, and we're starting to get working displays around the country. Because you put one of these things in, you press that control button, the little red light comes on: it's sold! Everybody loves it. And where it's gone in—a working display—it's become the leading product in that showroom almost immediately.

A Shift in Marketing Strategy?

The waitress began to clear the coffee cups. Rawlinson absently dusted at the crumbs on the tablecloth as he leaned forward and said:

> Once upon a time Microsoft was a tiny little provider of specialist software. Bill Gates had the vision to see that if you own the operating system on the PC, you can build from there. One of our presentations calls the Quartz the "Pentium Processor" because we can do so much once we have this kind of control over your bathroom ... we can use this technology with a shower ... but in the future we could use it with a bath, the sinks, whatever .... We're only limited by our creativity.

The question was, how to generate sales momentum? Was the problem that the Quartz was priced too high? Rawlinson wondered whether a discounted price might generate more market enthusiasm for his innovation. Because Quartz was such a breakthrough product, Rawlinson was loath to go this route. On the other hand, Rawlinson *was* willing to rethink his overall marketing strategy for the Quartz. Some of the marketing options he was debating included the following.

Targeting Consumers Directly

"We have so many problems reaching the plumbers," Rawlinson continued. "So I'm thinking to myself, why not target consumers with this product and try to build a consumer brand? Triton has proven that it can be done. And if there's ever been a breakthrough product to do it with, this is it. I think this is a 'bet the company' kind of product."

The problem with this option was that Rawlinson was finding it tough to justify a high-risk, high-reward strategy when company results were already healthy. As a test, a one-time-only print advertisement campaign was scheduled to run in *The Mail on Sunday* magazine in October (see **Exhibit 9** for copy of the advertisement). But, as Rawlinson noted, "One ad does not a campaign make. I'm not overly optimistic." A large-scale consumer campaign would cost about €3 million to €4 million over two years. With a net income of about €17 million, this would be a very tough sell across the company.

Targeting Do-It-Yourselfers

A second alternative was to target the do-it-yourself market. Rawlinson noted, "The Quartz is so easy to install, you or I could even do it." Aqualisa was currently selling its Gainsborough line to this market. The risk, as Rawlinson pointed out, was that "once you show up in the DIY sheds, you can't climb back out. You have to be careful about associating your premium brand with your discount channel."

On the other hand, the value proposition of the Quartz was so superior to that of the electric showers that dominated this market, [that] perhaps it *was* possible to charge a premium for this product through that channel, Rawlinson thought. In addition, he wondered if Aqualisa could get its partners like B&Q to help push the product, avoiding the need for expensive consumer advertising.

Targeting Developers

A third alternative was to target developers more aggressively. Rawlinson thought aloud: "The plus side is that this could conceivably be a large-volume channel. If we could get a couple of developers on board, we'd sell a lot of showers. In addition, it would force plumbers to get familiar with our product since they would have to install whatever the developers tell them to install." But there were downsides—including the significant time lag before showers would reach consumers through this route. As Rawlinson noted with some urgency, "We've got *at most* a two-year lead on the competition."

Rawlinson also wondered how tough a sell it would be to developers. Developers had already shown a reluctance to spend money on conventional Aqualisa products because they perceived those products to be premium brands; even at a 50% discount, the company had been unable to make the sale. And again, given that Quartz was such a breakthrough innovation, Rawlinson was reluctant to discount the price.

What to Do

If his managers were right and this was a niche product, Rawlinson wondered if maybe he should simply lower his expectations. Everything was basically well with the company—but at the same time, he could not help arguing:

> Business school taught me to think strategically, to be a visionary. Everything I learned at HBS tells me this is a breakthrough product. My worry is we'll miss the opportunity and in five years' time, someone else will have got the world market for this technology. We've had a nice, comfortable, contented life in the U.K., and it's hard to get a small company—particularly one that's been so profitable all these years—to be ambitious. But one of the things that a Harvard background gives you is the itch to think big. You see other companies that break out of the pack because they've got the right product and they've got the right vision. So why not this company?

Exhibit 1   The Aqualisa Organizational Chart

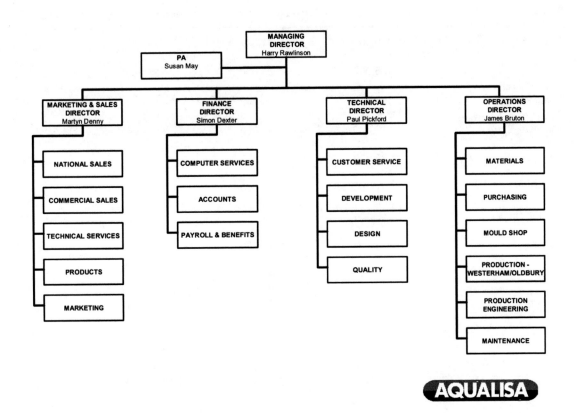

Source: Aqualisa.

Aqualisa Quartz: Simply a Better Shower   502-030

Exhibit 2   U.K. Market Share Data: Units Sold (2000)

Brand	Electric Showers	Mixer Showers	Power Showers	Total Units Sold
Triton	479,000	41,000	25,500	545,500
Mira	155,000	200,000	35,000	390,000
Gainsborough	180,000	20,500	3,000	203,500
Aqualisa	6,000	94,000	22,000	122,000
Masco	35,000	50,000	35,000	120,000
Ideal Standard	0	60,000	0	60,000
Heatrae Sadia	40,000	0	0	40,000
Bristan	0	20,000	0	20,000
Grohe	0	20,000	0	20,000
Hansgrohe	0	15,000	0	15,000
Others	205,000	29,500	29,500	264,000
Total Units Sold	**1,100,000**	**550,000**	**150,000**	**1,800,000**

Source: Aqualisa.

Exhibit 3   U.K. Shower Sales, by Reason for Installation

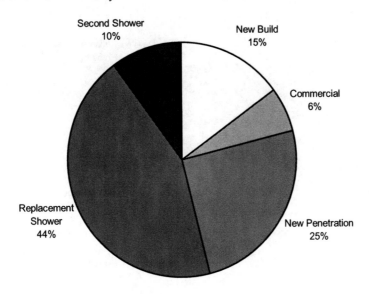

Source: Aqualisa.

Note: "New penetration" refers to new showers installed in existing bathrooms (where plumbing already exists—e.g., a shower added to a bathtub). "Second shower" refers to installation of a new shower in a location where no plumbing exists.

Exhibit 4   Shower Selection for Mixer Showers

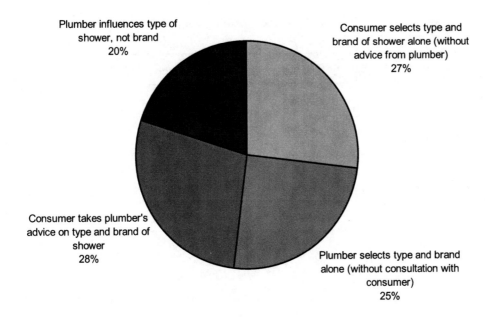

Source: Aqualisa.

Exhibit 5   U.K. Shower Market, by Installation Method (Mixer Showers Only)

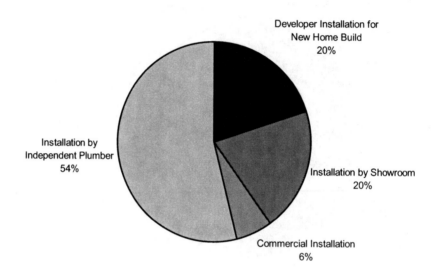

Developer Installation for New Home Build 20%

Installation by Showroom 20%

Commercial Installation 6%

Installation by Independent Plumber 54%

Source: Aqualisa.

Exhibit 6   U.K. Shower Market, by Product Type and Channel (Total Units Sold, 2000)

	Electric Showers	Mixer Showers	Power Showers
Do-It-Yourself Sheds	550,000	80,000	20,000
Showrooms	55,000	70,000	20,000
Trade Shops	330,000	400,000	110,000
Other (Electrical wholesalers)	165,000		
Total Units Sold	**1,100,000**	**550,000**	**150,000**

Source: Aqualisa.

Exhibit 7   Aqualisa Select Financials 2000 (€ in thousands)

Shower Sales (Electric, Mixer, Power, and Pumps)[a]	€46,212
Other[b]	21,744
Total Sales	**€67,956**
Gross Margins	**€31,824**
Sales	€4,080
Marketing	2,724
Customer Service	1,322
Research and Development	1,764
Finance, Administration & Depreciation	4,579
Total Overhead Spend	**€14,469**
Base Profit	**€17,355**

Source: Aqualisa.

[a] Includes all Aqualisa shower lines, including Aquastyle, Aquavalve, and Aquastream. Also includes Aqualisa pumps, as well as a variety of other specialty shower models sold by Aqualisa; these were primarily differentiated by style (e.g., contemporary, antique, brass, etc.). Does not include other brands such as ShowerMax and Gainsborough.

[b] Aqualisa sold a variety of other products, including shower accessories and commercial products.

Aqualisa Quartz: Simply a Better Shower   502-030

Exhibit 8   Aqualisa: Selected Products and Price Points

Model	Segment	Retail Price	MSP	Cost	Margin
Aquastyle	Premium	€230	€155	€95	€60
Aquavalve 609	Standard	€715	€380	€155	€225
Aquavalve Value	Value	€390	€205	€75	€130
Aquastream Thermostatic	Standard	€670	€350	€175	€175
Aquastream Manual	Value	€480	€250	€140	€110
Quartz Standard	Premium	€850	€450	€175	€275
Quartz Pumped	Premium	€1,080	€575	€230	€345
Aquaforce 1.0/1.5 Bar	Standard	€445	€230	€125	€105
Aquaforce 2.0/3.0 Bar	Premium	€595	€310	€175	€135

Source: Aqualisa.

Note: "Retail price" refers to the price charged by the retailer (trade shop, showroom, or DIY outlet) to the customer. "MSP" refers to manufacturer selling price (Aqualisa's price to the channel).

Exhibit 9   Advertisement for the Quartz Shower

Source: Aqualisa.

ZARA

Responsive, High Speed, Affordable Fashion

This case was prepared by Sophie Linguri under the supervision of Professor Nirmalya Kumar as a basis for classroom discussion rather than to illustrate either effective or ineffective handling of a management situation.

London Business
School reference
CS-05-037

Zara: Responsive, High-Speed, Affordable Fashion

In 1975, the first Zara store was opened in La Coruña, in Northwest Spain. By 2005, Zara's 723 stores had a selling area of 811,100 m^2 and occupied "privileged locations of major cities" in 56 countries. With sales of €3.8 billion in financial year 2004, Zara had become Spain's best-known fashion brand and the flagship brand of €5.7 billion holding group Inditex. Inditex's stock market listing in 2001 had turned Amancio Ortega, its founder and a self-made man, into the world's 23 richest man, with a personal fortune that *Forbes* magazine estimated at $12.6 billion.

Zara strived to deliver fashion apparel, often knock-offs of famous designers, at reasonable costs to young, fashion-conscious city-dwellers. Zara used in-house designers to present new items of clothing to customers twice a week, in response to sales and fashion trends. Thus the merchandise of any particular store was fresh and limited. To produce at such short notice required that Zara maintain a vertically integrated supply chain that distributed the clothes through a single state-of-the-art distribution centre. Unlike its competitors, 70-80% of Zara garments were manufactured in Europe.

In 2005, Pablo Isla was appointed the new Inditex chief executive. With plans to double the number of its stores by 2009, the rapid pace of growth was necessitating changes. First, Zara had opened a second distribution centre to increase capacity. Second, expanding into more distant markets meant that the number of items carried had increased to 12,000. Would Zara's business model be able to scale up? Or would the resulting complexity compromise its speed advantage? Would Pablo Isla be able to maintain the focus that Zara had established?

THE RETAIL APPAREL INDUSTRY AND COMPETITORS

The apparel industry was one of the most globalised industries, with 23.6 million workers in over 20 countries. As labour costs in Western European countries had risen, labour-intensive manufacturing operations had become increasingly outsourced to less developed countries. Hourly wages in the textile industry could be as low as 60 cents in India and China, compared with $2 in North Africa, $3 in Eastern Europe, $8.50 in Spain, and around $15.00 in Italy.

The 1974 *Multi-Fibre Arrangement*, which placed import quotas on garments and textiles from developing countries to the industrialised world, had expired on 1 January 2005 for all members of the World Trade Organization. This was amplifying the relocation of textile and garment manufacture to countries with lower labour costs, especially China. For example, in 2004, 400 Spanish textile groups went out of business, due to competition from Asia, resulting in the loss of 15,000 jobs. The Spanish textile guild predicted a loss of another 72,000 jobs by 2009.[1]

The apparel retail channels had consolidated during the 1990s, with a few large players dominating most major markets. Competitors included department stores, mass merchandisers (e.g. discounters and supermarkets) and specialty stores. Department stores were usually national players, like Marks & Spencer in the United Kingdom or Federated in the USA. Typically, they had lost market share in recent years. Mass merchandisers such as Target, Tesco and Wal-Mart had increasingly added private label clothes to their mix over the years to become major players. There were many successful specialty chains like Benetton, C&A, Hennes & Mauritz (referred to as H&M), The Limited, Mango and Next.

The traditional apparel industry model worked on long lead times (see *Exhibit 1*). The industry average was around nine months, around six months for design and three months for manufacturing. As a result, 45-60% of production was committed in the six-month pre-season period, with 80-100% committed by the start of the season. Only the remaining 0-20% was generally manufactured in-season in response to sales patterns. Excess inventory was marked down at the end of the season, and typically accounted for 30-40% of sales. Despite their best efforts, Zara's closest competitors, H&M and Gap, still took around five months to produce new clothing lines.

H&M

Swedish clothing chain H&M was founded in 1947. By 2005, it had close to 32,000 employees, just under 1,100 stores in 20 countries. In 2005, it planned to open 155 new stores in Europe and the US. Its 2004 sales were €6 billion, which yielded a profit of 1.24 billion. With close to 30% of its sales, Germany was H&M's largest market, while the US generated only

Iman for H&M Germany

6.4% of its 2004 sales. It manufactured 60% of its clothes in Asia.

H&M's business concept was to offer fashion and quality at the best price. In order to offer the latest fashion, H&M had its own buying and design department. It claimed to achieve the best price by:
- Few middlemen
- Buying in large volumes
- Having a broad, in-depth knowledge of design, fashion, and textiles
- Buying the right products from the right market
- Being cost conscious at every stage
- Having efficient distribution

H&M's clothing lines in men's wear, women's wear and children's wear, as well as its cosmetics range, targeted cost-conscious shoppers. Within H&M women's wear were different sub-brands: Hennes (women aged 25-35), L.O.G.G. (casual sportswear), Impuls (young women's trends), BiB (plus-size line), Woman (classic), Clothes (current trends), MAMA (maternity) and Rocky (youth fashion). There were also different sub-brands within the men's and children's lines.

H&M stores generally had a somewhat chaotic, marketplace feel, with clothes packed tightly onto racks, frequent markdowns, and queues at the cash register. H&M devoted 5% of its revenues to advertising. Its high-profile ad campaigns featured celebrities, such as Claudia Schiffer, Johnny Depp, Naomi Campbell and Jerry Hall, wearing its low-cost clothes. Dedicated collections by star designers Karl Lagerfeld and Stella McCartney in 2004-5 continued to create buzz among its customers.

The Gap

Madonna for Gap

Gap opened its first store in San Francisco in 1969, where it sold mainly Levis jeans. In 1991, Gap announced its decision to sell only private label brands. With around 3,000 stores and 152,000 employees worldwide, Gap positioned itself as a provider of high quality, basic items, such as jeans, khakis and t-shirts. In addition to Old Navy and Banana Republic, Gap's chains included GapBody, GapKids, and babyGap. Its 2004 sales were around €12.5 billion, with a profit of $1.4 billion. Nearly all of Gap's products were manufactured outside the US, with 18% of its collection made in China.

Gap's stores were spacious, with stock well spaced and neatly presented. There was an emphasis on service, with a call button in fitting rooms for customers requiring assistance with clothing sizes. Television advertisements featured hip music and dance sequences, with appearances by celebrities such as Madonna, Lenny Kravitz, Sarah Jessica Parker and Joss Stone.

INDITEX HISTORY

Spanish entrepreneur Amancio Ortega Gaona started a firm manufacturing lingerie and nightwear in 1963, after quitting his job as a runner for a shirtmaker in La Coruña. He founded Confecciones GOA in 1972, and opened the first Zara store in 1975, to sell stock after a customer cancelled a large order.

**Aamancio Ortega Gaona
Inditex Chairman**

Ortega founded the Inditex group in 1985. After floating 26% of its shares on the Madrid stock exchange in 2001, he remained its majority shareholder, with 61% of the company's shares. Ortega retained a low profile, rarely making public appearances (apart from during the run-up to the IPO in 2000), and had never given an interview.

José María Castellano Ríos joined Inditex in 1985 and became its Chief Executive in 1997. Castellano had previously been IT manager of Aegon España SA, and had a doctorate in economics and business studies. In 2005, Inditex developed a five-year plan, which included a board restructure. As part of the restructure, Pablo Isla Álvarez de Tejera was appointed as Chief Executive in May 2005. Isla came from the Franco-Spanish tobacco group Altadis, where he had been co-chairman. Isla was chosen for his experience in international distribution. Ortega stayed on as the group's Chairman, and Castellano remained the Deputy Chairman.

Portfolio of Stores

Besides Zara, which was targeted at trendy city youngsters, Inditex grew its portfolio of apparel chains throughout the 1990s. Each chain was targeted at a specific segment (see *Exhibit 2*):

- Massimo Dutti – Young businessmen
- Pull & Bear - Elegant male clothing
- Berksha – Elegant fashion for young women
- Brettos – Trendy young suburban women
- Oysho – Lingerie
- Stradivarius – Youthful fashion
- Kiddy's Class – Trendy children

In 2003, Inditex opened a home furnishings chain called Zara Home. By 2005, Zara made up close to 70% of Inditex sales and led the group's international expansion (see *Exhibit 3*). While, as a group, Inditex had about twice the number of stores as H&M, Zara's 700 stores were fewer in number than H&M's. Inditex was aggressively expanding, and planned to increase its 2,000 stores to 4,000 by 2009, in Europe, Asia, and the U.S. (see *Exhibit 4*). In terms of profits, Inditex was performing well compared with its main competitor, H&M (see *Exhibit 5* and *Exhibit 6*).

THE ZARA STORE

91% of Zara stores were company-owned; the rest were franchises or joint ventures. Customers entering a Zara store on Regent Street in London, Rue Rivoli in Paris, Fifth Avenue in New York or Avenidas das Americas in Rio de Janeiro generally found themselves in the same environment: a predominantly white, modern and spacious store, well-lit and walled with mirror. The latest fashions hung from the store racks around them. A long line of people typically waited at the cash registers to pay for their purchases: a few select items.

**Shop Window of Zara,
New York**

In comparison with other clothing retailers, who spent 3-4% of sales on advertising, Zara spent just 0.3%. The little it did spend went to reinforce its identity as a clothing retailer that was low-cost but high fashion (see *Exhibit 7*). Instead Zara concentrated on creating compelling store windows and to the design of its shops, which had won awards. It relied on its shop windows, which were dramatically lit and used neutral backgrounds, to communicate its brand image. The shop windows of Zara stores were changed regularly, according to display designs sent by headquarters, and were critical for Zara to remain visible and entice customers. Store locations were carefully researched to determine that there was a sufficiently large customer base for Zara[2], and as such were generally busy, prestigious, city centre shopping streets.

Zara was a fashion imitator. It focussed its attention on understanding what fashion items its customers wanted and then delivering them, rather than on promoting predicted season's trends via fashion shows and similar channels of influence, that the fashion industry traditionally used. Its 200 in-house designers were trend-spotters who kept their finger on the fashion pulse, and translated trends into styles that were universally accessible. At Zara headquarters in La Coruña, store specialists (who were responsible for a number of stores in a region) worked closely with designers to develop styles that would work for different markets. Collections were renewed every year, with an average of 11,000 styles produced annually, compared with the more typical collections of 2,000-4,000 produced annually by rivals H&M and Gap.

Production and distribution of new clothing pieces was favoured over replenishing existing items, contributing to the perception of scarcity cultivated in Zara stores. Customers returned frequently to stores, to browse new items. The global average of 17 visits per customer per year for Zara was considerably higher than the three visits to its competitors.[3] Visitors were also more likely to purchase, as one senior executive explained:

> Zara's objective is not that consumers buy a lot but that they buy often and will find something new every time they enter the store.[4]

Comments by Luis Blanc, and Inditex director, illustrated how Zara stores fostered an environment of immediacy:

> We want our customers to understand that if they like something, they must buy it now, because it won't be in the shops the following week. It is all about creating a climate of scarcity and opportunity.[5]

Affordable prices helped to encourage purchases, and Zara's offering was often referred to as clothing to be worn six to ten times.

Zara's pricing differed across country markets. It set prices according to individual market conditions, rather than using cost plus margin as its basis (which was the formula used by most of its competitors). In Spain, Zara products were low-cost, while in the US, Japan and Mexico, they were priced as a luxury fashion item. Prices in France were somewhat higher than in Spain, since the average French consumer was willing to pay more for fashion than most other European consumers. For example, in 2003, the price of jeans in Zara stores in France was $34.58 compared with $24.87 in Spain and $54 in Japan.[6] Until 2002, Zara had used one price tag listing the price in different currencies, to simplify tagging of items. In 2002, however, it implemented a system of local pricing, using a bar code reader that printed the correct local price for items.

Compared with its competitors, Zara generally priced its products somewhat higher than C&A and H&M, but below Gap, Next and Kookai. For example, a similar shirt cost $26 at Zara, compared with a price of $29 at Gap and $9 at H&M.[7]

Store Management

Zara Store, Barcelona

Store managers were encouraged to run their store like a small business. Salespeople were well trained, and Zara promoted its people from within as much as possible. Store managers' remuneration was partially dependent on the accuracy of their sales forecasts and sales growth.[8] Each evening a handheld PDA displayed the newest designs sent by headquarters, which were available for order. Order deadlines were twice weekly, and were issued via the handhelds. Store managers who failed to order by the deadline received replenishment items only.

Store managers regularly spoke with store specialists, who also received real time sales data from stores, to discuss which items were selling well or if customers had requested specific items. This information was then fed back to the design process.[9] Deliveries arrived at stores twice per week from Zara headquarters, a few days after the order was made, and contained both replenishment items as well as new products. Headquarters also sometimes included products that had not been ordered, which stores expected to receive. If demand of an item exceeded supply, some stores did not receive the product they had ordered. Zara also tested some of its products in limited numbers in its test stores, before introducing them on a wider scale. Failure rates of Zara's new products were reported to be just 1%, considerably lower than the industry average of 10%.[10]

Technology was a key part of enabling communications and information flow. While information technology was fundamental to its business, its IT infrastructure was relatively simple (even dated by some standards), which meant that Zara's IT expenditure was significantly lower than its rivals (as much as five to ten times lower).[11] Deputy Chairman José María Castellano explained the key role played by technology:

> Technology in this company is important and will be more important in the future. The technology we use is mainly information technology and [enables] the communication between the shop managers and the design team here in headquarters.[12]

THE ZARA SUPPLY CHAIN

Around 50% of Zara's garments were sourced from third parties. Unlike its competitors, Zara's outsourced production came for the most part from Europe (60%), with just 27% coming from Asia, and another 10% from the rest of the world. The products sourced from Asia were basic collection items or wardrobe "staples," with minimum fashion content, such as T-shirts, lingerie and woollens, and where there was a clear cost advantage. Formal contracts were kept to a minimum, and Zara was generally a preferred customer due to its order volume and stability.[13] Externally manufactured items were shipped to Zara's distribution centre. Zara intended to source more of the collection from Asia in the future, as commented by Castellano: "In the next few years, we will source more basic items from China and Vietnam, but the high value added fashion items will continue to be made closer to home."[14]

The other 50% of Zara's garments, those that were more fashion-dependent, were manufactured in-house, in more than 20 Zara factories located in nearby Arteixo.[15] For its in-house manufacturing, it purchased fabric from Comditel, a subsidiary of Inditex. Half of this fabric was purchased grey (undyed) to enable Zara to respond to changes in colour trends during the season. Dye was purchased from Fibracolor, in which Inditex held a stake.

A team of 200 young, talented yet unknown designers were hired (often recent graduates of top design schools) to create designs, based on the latest fashions from the catwalk and other fashion hotspots, which were easily translatable to the mass market.[16] Working alongside the market specialists and production planners, designers for each of Zara's collections (Woman, Man, Child) kept in-touch with market developments, to create around 40,000 new designs per year, of which around one-quarter were manufactured.[17] The design and production working environment was consistent with Zara's flat hierarchical structure, in which prima donnas were not tolerated.[18]

Illustration: Fast Fashion

Crown Prince Felipe of Spain and Letizia Ortiz Rocasolano

Zara was a master of picking up up-to-the-minute trends and churning them out to stores around the world in a matter of weeks.

• After Madonna's first concert date in Spain during a recent tour, her outfit was copied by Zara designers. By the time she performed her last concert in Spain, some members of the audience were wearing the same outfit.

• In 2003, when the Crown Prince of Spain announced his engagement to Letizia Ortiz Rocasolano, she wore a white trouser-suit for the occasion (pictured left). In just a few weeks, the same white trouser-suit was hanging from Zara's clothes racks all over Europe, where it was snatched up by the ranks of the fashion-conscious.

Computers were used to guide the cutting tools, using patterns made from selected designs. Zara tried to keep its offering of any style simple, usually in three sizes and three colours only. The labour intensive sewing of the garments was outsourced to around 500 local subcontractors, who used seamstresses in cooperatives. Zara was usually their sole client, and they worked without any written contracts. Zara paid these subcontractors a flat fee per type of garment, (e.g., €5 for a pair of trousers and €15 per jacket) and they were expected to operate on short lead times and fast turnaround. Subcontractors picked up the prepared fabric pieces from Zara, and returned them to the 500,000 m^2 distribution centre.[19]

At the Zara distribution centre, optical reading devices were used to sort and distribute over 60,000 items per hour. The garments were then picked up and transported by truck to different destinations all over Europe (which made up about 75% of deliveries). Products for more distant destinations were transported by air (about 25%). Throughout the process, garments were tracked using bar codes. Shipments tended to have almost zero flaws, with 98.9% accuracy and under 0.5% shrinkage.[20]

Since Zara's garments were produced in-house, it was able to make a new line from start to finish in just three weeks (see *Exhibit 8*). This varied somewhat depending on the type of garment: new garments took about five weeks from design to store delivery, while revamped existing items could take as little as two weeks. As a result Zara could be responsive to fashion items that were selling well during the season, and to discontinue those that were not. By constantly refreshing the collection, and manufacturing items in high-intensity, short-runs, Zara was able to prevent the accumulation of non-saleable inventories.

It was estimated that Zara committed just 15-25% of production before the season began, 50 to 60% at the start of the season, and the remainder manufactured in-season. Percentage of Zara sales consisting of markdowns was 15-20%. In some cases, stores ran out of stock. However, this was not viewed as a negative since it contributed to customers' perception of the uniqueness of their purchase: "Customers are actually satisfied to see items out of stock as they are then confident that there is little chance that many other customers will wear the same dress."[21]

Castellano explained the rationale for this departure from industry norms:

> We don't want to compete in the bottom end of the market. We offer fashion with a high design content.

> If I tried to source my collections in Asia, I would not be able to get them quickly enough to our stores. By manufacturing close to home, I can scrap collections when they are not selling. And without this rapid response, I would not be able to extract a good relation between quality, price and fashion which is what our customers have come to expect.[22]

A study in 2000 estimated that Zara managed to generate 14.7% operating margins as a percentage of sales, compared with 10.6% for Gap and 12.3% for H&M. Additionally, the same study put Zara's inventory turnover at 10.67 outpacing Gap at 7.18 and H&M at 6.84.[23]

THE FUTURE

Following Zara's success, competitors sought to reduce their own lead times. The competitive advantage achieved by Zara's vertical integration appeared to be eroding. With its highly centralised structure and its rapid growth, Zara was producing around 12,000 different items per year by 2005. As it opened stores in increasingly distant markets, would Zara be able to retain its flexibility in adjusting production to accommodate differences in local trends? Would the increase in complexity result in a need to create regional production facilities? How would this affect the advantage Zara gained from its centralization?

Might Chinese clothing manufacturers prove to be a competitive threat to Zara, with their high capacity and continuous improvements in quality? Castellano discounted this threat: "Being a Zara or Gap is not just about designing fashionable clothes and manufacturing them cheaply. You must also make the transition to being a retailer. It is a big step from manufacturing to distribution. There is also the question of managing the location and presentation of stores, training staff and so on."[24]

The Zara model seemed to work better in markets where customers had an appetite for fashion (such as France, Italy, Japan and the UK). However, in countries such as France and Italy, Zara had received bad press for copying designs from couture labels, and the French Fashion Federation had called for limited access by reporters to fashion shows to minimize imitation by copycatters. In other markets, where consumers were less fashion-focussed (e.g. Germany and the U.S.A.) Zara seemed somewhat less successful. Would Zara be better served in the long run by increasing penetration in these fashion-sensitive markets, or by extending its global reach through increased presence in more markets?

Exhibit 1: Traditional Season for a High Street Store

ID	Task	Duration
1	Range Concept, Fabric Selection	51 days
2	Design Presentation & Feedback	16 days
3	Buying Plan Approval, Fabric Booking	31 days
4	Fabric Tests, Lab Dips, Etc	46 days
5	Prototype Development, Approval, Final Specs	56 days
6	Garment Vendor, PO, Size set sample	51 days
7	Production, Bar Codes, Packaging	91 days
8	Shipment	5 days

Timeline: 13 Sep '04 – 29 Aug '05

Adapted from Dutta, 2004[25]

140

Exhibit 2: Inditex Stores and Sales

Sales, by Division (2004-5)

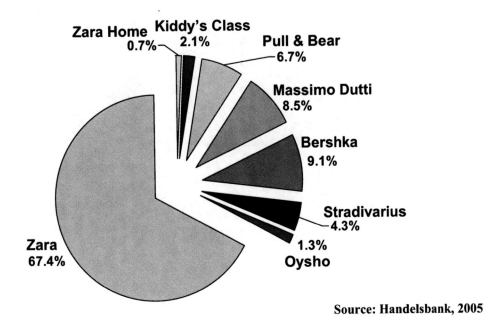

Source: Handelsbank, 2005

Percentage of Stores (2005)

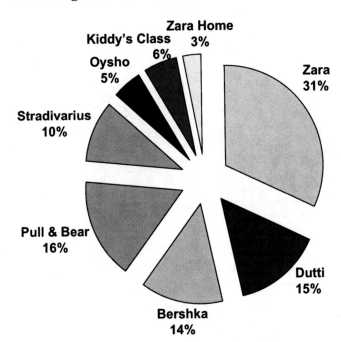

Source: Financial Times, 2005

Exhibit 3: Number of Zara Stores by Country (31 March 2005)

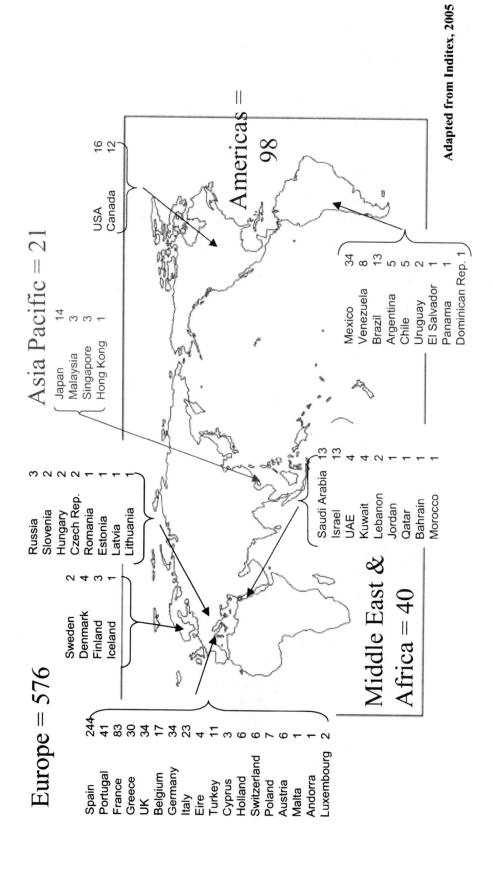

Europe = 576

Spain	244
Portugal	41
France	83
Greece	30
UK	34
Belgium	17
Germany	34
Italy	23
Eire	4
Turkey	11
Cyprus	3
Holland	6
Switzerland	6
Poland	7
Austria	6
Malta	1
Andorra	1
Luxembourg	2

Sweden	2
Denmark	4
Finland	3
Iceland	1

Russia	3
Slovenia	2
Hungary	2
Czech Rep.	2
Romania	1
Estonia	1
Latvia	1
Lithuania	1

Asia Pacific = 21

Japan	14
Malaysia	3
Singapore	3
Hong Kong	1

Americas = 98

USA	16
Canada	12

Mexico	34
Venezuela	8
Brazil	13
Argentina	5
Chile	5
Uruguay	2
El Salvador	1
Panama	1
Dominican Rep.	1

Middle East & Africa = 40

Saudi Arabia	13
Israel	13
UAE	4
Kuwait	4
Lebanon	2
Jordan	1
Qatar	1
Bahrain	1
Morocco	1

Adapted from Inditex, 2005

Exhibit 4: Inditex Store Formats

	Zara		Kiddy's Class		Pull & Bear		Massimo Dutti		Bershka		Stradivarius		Oysho		Zara Home	
	2004	2003	2004	2003	2004	2003	2004	2003	2004	2003	2004	2003	2004	2003	2004	2003
No of stores	723	626	129	103	371	350	327	297	302	253	227	191	104	76	62	26
Turnover*	3,820	3,220	121	90	379	288	481	389	516	395	242	162	72	45	40	11
Operating Income*	648	476	22	18.0	56	19	75	60	83	57	39	4	16	2	0.3	(0.5)
% international sales	65.8	63.5	12.8	13.4	30.5	31	41.9	40.9	35.7	33.8	15.4	16.6	31.5	35.1	12.7	8.5
% of Inditex	67.4	70	2.1	1.9	6.7	6.3	8.5	8.5	9.1	8.6	4.3	3.5	1.3	1	0.7	0.2
ROCE	38%	33%	61%	80%	44%	16%	50%	56%	52%	46%	43%	5%	52%	7%	2%	--

*in millions of Euros, rounded off.

Source: Inditex press dossier, 2005

Exhibit 5: Key Indicators of Gap, H&M and Inditex (Financial Years 2003 & 2004)

	Gap[i]		H&M		Inditex	
Reporting Date	29 January 2005[ii]	29 January 2004[iii]	30 November 2004[iv]	30 November 2003[v]	31 January 2005	31 January 2004
Sales (millions €)	12,470	12,696	6,029	5,330	5,670	4,599
Gross Profit (millions €)	4,892	4,780	3,449	2,994	3,034	2,306
Operating Profit (millions €)	1,598	1,522	1,198	1,019	925	627
Profit (millions €)	1,435	1,349	1,236	1,062	886	613
Profit after tax (millions €)	882	826	817	706	628	446
Total Assets (millions €)	7,703	8,579	3,159	2,847	4,209	3,510
Inventories (millions €)	1,390	1,365	577	558	514	486
Stores	2,994	3,022	1,068	945	2,244	1,922
Employees	152,000	150,000	31,701	28,409	47,046	39,760
Countries	5	6	20	18	56	48
Total square metres (thousands)	3,399	3,393	1,364[vi]	n/a	1,175	988

Source: Inditex, H&M and Gap, 2005

---

[i] Gap Inc's stores include Gap, Old Navy and Banana Republic. Gap's sales were €5.6 million, with 1643 stores, and 1.43 million square metres.

[ii] Exchange Rate of 29 January 2005 is used for all currency calculations: 0.76660 USD = 1€

[iii] Exchange Rate of 29 January 2004 is used for all currency calculations 0.80080 USD = €1

[iv] Exchange Rate of 30 November 2004 is used for all currency calculations 0.11230 SEK = 1€

[v] Exchange Rate of 30 November 2003 is used for all currency calculations 0.11050 SEK = 1€

[vi] Estimated (Adapted from Datamonitor, 2005).

Exhibit 6: Iniditex vs. H&M (1998-2004)

Sales, Inditex vs H&M (Millions, €)

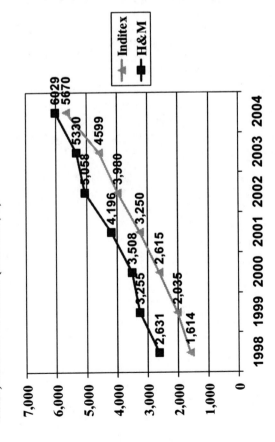

Number of Stores, Inditex vs H&M (1999-2004)

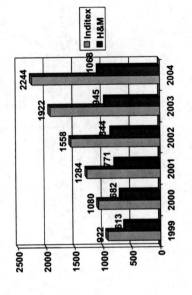

Number of Countries, Inditex vs H&M (1999-2004)

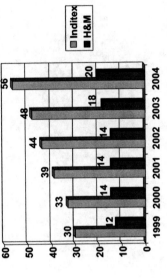

Adapted from Inditex and H&M, 2005

......

Exhibit 7: A Zara advertisement

The Cheap
Frock coat (119)
White shirt (25) ZARA
Black necktie (65) HACKETT
Woollen Trousers (45) and
Black boots (55), both ZARA

The Expensive
Black cashmere frock coat (950)
White tuxedo shirt (190)
Black necktie (86) and
Woollen Trousers (380) both
RALPH LAUREN
Black boots (500) are by UNGARO

Exhibit 8: Zara Season

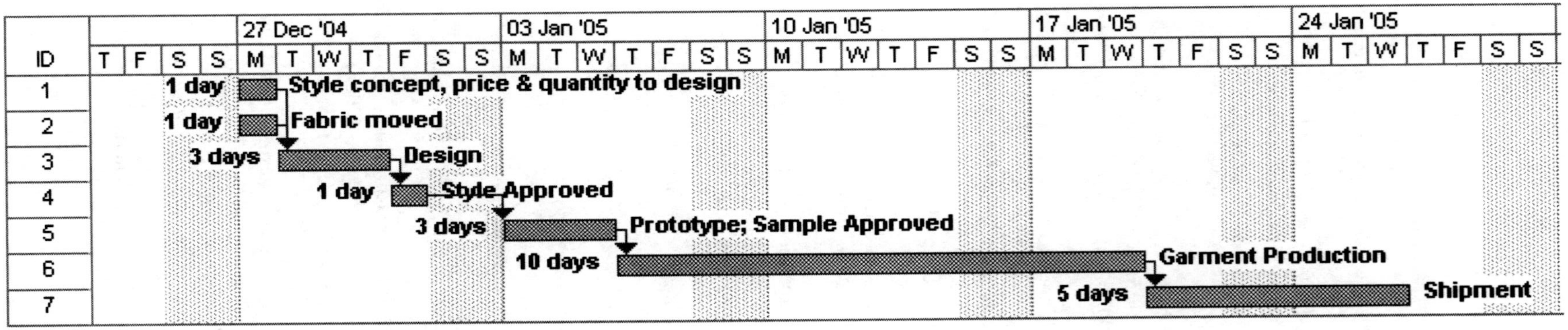
ID
27 Dec '04
03 Jan '05
10 Jan '05
17 Jan '05
24 Jan '05
1 day Style concept, price & quantity to design
1 day Fabric moved
3 days Design
1 day Style Approved
3 days Prototype; Sample Approved
10 days Garment Production
5 days Shipment

Adapted from Dutta, 2004

Endnotes

[1] Crawford, L. (2005) "Inditex sizes up Europe in expansion drive," *Financial Times*, 1 February 2005, p. 30.

[2] Ferdows, K.J., A.D. Machuca and M. Lewis (2003) "Zara," *CIBER Case Collection*, Indiana University.

[3] D'Andrea, G. and D. Arnold (2003) "Zara," *Harvard Business School Case* 9-503-050, p.7.

[4] "Zara, la déferlante de la mode espagnole," Interview with Stéphane Labelle, MD of Zara France, *Enjeux-Les Echos*, February 1996.

[5] Crawford, L. (2000) "Inside Track: Putting on the style with rapid response," *Financial Times*, 26 February 2000.

[6] D'Andrea, G. and D. Arnold (2003) "Zara," *Harvard Business School Case* 9-503-050, p.19.

[7] D'Andrea, G. and D. Arnold (2003) "Zara," *Harvard Business School Case* 9-503-050, p.18

[8] Ferdows, K.J., K.M. Lewis and J.A.D. Machuca (2003) "Zara," *Supply Chain Forum* 4(2): 62.

[9] Ferdows, K.J., A.D. Machuca and M. Lewis (2003) "Zara," *CIBER Case Collection*, Indiana University, p.6.

[10] Ghemawat, P. and J.L. Nueno (2003) "Zara: Fast Fashion," *Harvard Business School Case* 9-703-497, p.10.

[11] "The Future of Fast Fashion," *The Economist*, 18 June 2005, p.63.

[12] "Zara: A Retailer's Dream," from http://www.fashionunited.co.uk/news/archive/inditex1.htm <accessed 3 June 2005>

[13] Ferdows, K.J., A.D. Machuca and M. Lewis (2003) "Zara," *CIBER Case Collection*, Indiana University, p.7.

[14] Crawford, L. (2005) "Inditex sizes up Europe in expansion drive," *Financial Times*, 1 February 2005, p. 30.

[15] Fraiman, N., M. Singh, L. Arrington and C. Paris (2002) "Zara," *Columbia Business School Case*, p. 5.

[16] Ghemawat, P. and J.L. Nueno (2003) "Zara: Fast Fashion," *Harvard Business School Case* 9-703-497, p.10.

[17] Fraiman, N., M. Singh, L. Arrington and C. Paris (2002) "Zara," *Columbia Business School Case*, p. 5.

[18] Ferdows, K.J., A.D. Machuca and M. Lewis (2003) "Zara," *CIBER Case Collection*, Indiana University, p.6.

[19] Fraiman, N., M. Singh, L. Arrington and C. Paris (2002) "Zara," *Columbia Business School Case*, p. 6.

[20] Ferdows, K.J., A.D. Machuca and M. Lewis (2003) "Zara," *CIBER Case Collection*, Indiana University, p.8.

[21] Interview with Anthony Pralle, Senior Vice President of Boston Consulting Group, Madrid, 13 July 1999, as quoted in Harle, N., M. Pich and L. Van der Heyden (2002) "Marks & Spencer and Zara: Process Competition in the Textile Apparel Industry," *INSEAD Case* 602-010-1.

[22] Crawford, L. "Inditex sizes up Europe in expansion drive: Rapid design, manufacture and distribution keep pressure on rivals," *Financial Times*, 1 February 2005.

[23] D'Andrea, G. and D. Arnold (2003) "Zara," *Harvard Business School Case* 9-503-050.

[24] Crawford, L. (2005) "Inditex sizes up Europe in expansion drive," *Financial Times*, 1 February 2005, p. 30.

[25] Dutta, D. (2004) "Brand Watch: Zara," *Images Fashion Forum Presentation*, New Delhi, 12 February 2004.